&Bull

Very soon we hope to be riding desegrated buses:

In order that this transition may take place peaceably and without violence, we offer the following, as Rules of Conduct on Buses:

1. Avoid all possible friction.

    A. If you are pushed, do not push back.

    B. If someone strike you, do not return the blow. (Remember, We are Christians and Leaders)

    C. Never argue with anyone, irrespective of race.

2. The most important rule about conduct in public is:

BE QUIET...REFRAIN FROM BOISTEROUS LAUGHTER AND LOUD TALKING BE COURTEOUS

3. Watch your conversation... Do not converse with anyone unless it is necessary.... and then, if you must:

Don't be loud
Don't use profane language
Confine your conversation to your friend, with whom you are sharing the seat... talk to him in a soft tone
Confine your conversation to world affairs. Leave off the talk of your personal and racial affairs until you arrive at your home..... NEVER discuss controversial affairs on public conveyances.... NEVER discuss the problems with your employers (**What you said and what she said**)

4. Eat your meals at home not on the bus

Don't allow your children to even eat candy bars They criticize us for eating on the streets and busses and then throwing the wrappers, peanuts shells and other rubbish everywhere but in containers provided for that purpose ... No one wants your child's sticky hands on him or the seat on which he is to sit.

5. Be sure your clothes and body are always clean

Most jobs provide facilities for getting clean before starting home

Regardless to your tiredness refrain from sitting next to someone when your clothes are dirty

6. Make and accept an apology readily and pleasantly If by chance You step on another's toes or brush against another...make an apology.

7. Don't sprawl in your seat with your feet blocking the aisle.

8. Find a vacant seat whenever possible

9. Read your newspaper or a book while traveling

Reading will not only profit you, but it will keep us out of so much conversation and the trouble of looking at someone too much. Read if you have to read the pictures

10. Remember to be courteous at all times

Black & White

The Confrontation between Reverend Fred L. Shuttlesworth and Eugene "Bull" Connor

Larry Dane
BRIMNER

CALKINS CREEK
Honesdale, Pennsylvania

For information about permission to
reproduce selections from this book, please
contact permissions@highlights.com.

Calkins Creek
An Imprint of Boyds Mills Press, Inc.
815 Church Street
Honesdale, Pennsylvania 18431
Printed in the United States of
America

ISBN: 978-1-59078-766-3

Library of Congress Control Number:
2011924006

First edition

Book design by Bill Anton | Service
Station

10 9 8 7 6 5 4 3 2 1

In the spring of 1963, ACMHR
members and supporters launched a
series of protests aimed at publicizing
the segregation practices—in terms
of both hiring and service—of
Birmingham's five department stores.
Commissioner Eugene "Bull" Connor
(foreground) issues a warning that
the protesters will be arrested.

For the ACMHR foot soldiers,
and for Susan Campbell Bartoletti, who inspires

—L.D.B

CONTENTS

The Preacher   6

The Commissioner   38

Confrontation   50

AUTHOR'S NOTE   102

FOR FURTHER INFORMATION   105

ACKNOWLEDGMENTS   105

SOURCE NOTES   106

INDEX   108

PICTURE CREDITS   109

The Preacher

"I have a feeling that my life, for some reason, is designed to touch many people."

—REVEREND FRED L. SHUTTLESWORTH

The Ku Klux Klan was born in Pulaski, Tennessee, shortly after the end of the Civil War. The first night rides of the members, dressed in robes and hoods, may have been innocent enough. However, they soon turned to violence as the Klan adopted an attitude of white superiority and worked to intimidate Negroes in order to deprive them of full equality. In this 1948 photo, Dr. Samuel Green, Georgia Grand Dragon of the KKK, and others protest President Harry Truman's civil rights program.

**he first time** the Ku Klux Klan (KKK) tried to kill Reverend Fred L. Shuttlesworth was Christmas 1956. The KKK was a group that believed white people were superior to Negroes. Its members intimidated blacks—and whites who supported the Negro quest for equality and justice—through threats and violence.

Christmas should have been a joyful time for Fred and his family. But he was a preacher who believed "like Moses [that] people ought to have the opportunity to try to be free." For Fred, freedom without the limitations and restrictions imposed on Negroes was a black-and-white issue—one either was or was not free. And freedom meant equality under the law. Because of this, he became a favorite target of Alabama's KKK.

That morning, Fred preached his Christmas sermon. It was peppered with remarks about upcoming actions to protest racial segregation—or separation—in the city of Birmingham. Afterward he visited his oldest daughter, Pat, who was in the hospital following an accident earlier in the morning. While lighting the gas heater, she'd gotten too close and her robe caught fire. Thinking quickly, Fred wrapped her in a blanket, extinguishing the flames, but Pat was burned. His wife, Ruby, and a neighbor rushed her to the hospital, where she remained for several weeks. After visiting with his daughter, he returned home to spend time with Ruby and their three other children: Ricky, Fred Jr., and Carolyn. Christmas had been anything but joyful, and more turmoil lay in store for the preacher and his family.

In the evening, Charlie Robinson, a church deacon, and his wife paid their Christmas respects. With Fred, however, any visit was seldom purely social.

The freedom fighter and his children (from left to right): Carolyn, Patricia, Reverend Fred L. Shuttlesworth, Fred Jr., and Ricky.

So while the women and children were talking in another part of the house, he and the deacon went into the front bedroom to discuss the civil rights protest action that was planned for the next day. Then without warning, a thunderous blast ripped through the house, and the walls tumbled down. It was about 9:40 p.m.

Fred was born Freddie Lee Robinson on March 18, 1922, in the rural farming community of Mount Meigs, Alabama. His family—mother, Alberta; maternal grandparents, March and Martha; and Alberta's seven siblings—earned a meager living raising corn and cotton and keeping some chickens and livestock. Fred never knew much of Mount Meigs. When he was three, his grandfather decided to move the large Robinson clan to Oxmoor, a mining community ten miles southwest of Birmingham. Jobs in the mines didn't pay Negroes much, but they paid better than farming. But March had another reason for the move—to end Alberta's relationship with Fred's father, Vetter Greene. March thought Greene unsuitable for his daughter despite the arrival of a second child, a girl named Cleola, or Cleo.

When Fred was almost five, his mother met and married William "Will" Nathan Shuttlesworth. Alberta taught her children that the man who provided for them was their father. So Fred and Cleo adopted Will's name. The family would eventually include seven other brothers and sisters—a total of three boys and six girls.

Alberta Robinson Shuttlesworth (1900–1995), Fred's mother, at her home in Oxmoor, Alabama, around 1930.

Strong-willed, Alberta was the family disciplinarian. She accidentally lost her right eye in a wrangle with her husband, Will.

As the 1930s ushered in the Great Depression—a period of high unemployment, long soup lines, and profound homelessness and hopelessness in the United States—the Shuttlesworths at least had a roof over their heads. Will and a friend had built the house for the family to live in, but it had no running water or electricity. Eight-year-old Fred and his younger brother Eugene hauled drinking water from a well and washing water from a spring. The Shuttlesworths also had a small plot of land that Fred helped to plow with a mule so they could grow "[c]orn, 'tatoes, peas . . . everything."

His mother was a dominant influence on Fred and set the course that he would follow throughout his life. Alberta had been raised in a church-going family of Methodists, and she insisted that her children attend church with her every week. As Fred explained, "My mother never did allow me the luxury

"If I got a whipping at school, I got another one at home."

of being asked whether I wanted to go to church. In fact, she would assist me if I wasn't out of the bed on time by a strap or whip or whatever. I had to go." But he enjoyed the sermons "about the supernatural"—about God—and the more he listened to them, the more he thought about becoming a preacher.

Fred's wife, Ruby Keeler Shuttlesworth, pictured here later in life, stood with Fred in his many battles for racial equality.

Strong of will, Alberta also was the family disciplinarian. "She didn't have much," Fred remembered, "but . . . she insisted that we obey. If I got a whipping at school, I got another one at home." Despite this, Fred had a prankish nature. Once, when he got in trouble for talking in class, his teacher made him stand in the corner for punishment. When she wasn't looking, he moved the hands of the nearby clock ahead a few minutes. This pleased some of the girls in class, and they rewarded him with their smiles. So the next time his teacher wasn't looking, he moved the hands of the clock ahead a little more. Eventually, the clock said three o'clock— dismissal time. His teacher rang the bell, but then quickly discovered her mistake. Forty-five minutes still remained in the school day! Embarrassed, she called the students back to their seats. She took Fred to the cloakroom and whipped him with a leather strap. But when they came out, his teacher caught Fred smiling at the girls. It made her so angry that she took him back to the cloakroom and whipped him again. She did this four times—until Fred thought he'd better stop smiling.

In May 1940, Fred graduated from high school near the top of his class. He was eighteen years old. He took a job with a group of doctors in Birmingham where he helped elderly patients and also boiled needles to sterilize them. While there, Fred met a fellow worker who would change his life—Ruby Keeler, a nursing student at Tuskegee Institute.

Tuskegee was founded by Booker T. Washington in 1881 to teach Negroes technical skills that would help them improve their economic and social lives. Fred liked Ruby's company and soon began walking her home. Occasionally, they took in a movie together or went to church. The couple married on October 20, 1941. Ruby never returned to Tuskegee.

Just before he and Ruby were married, Fred found a better-paying job at the Alpha Portland Cement Plant, where he earned fifty-four cents an hour. He shoveled rock at the quarry, a pit where limestone was dug from the ground. Ruby continued to work for the group of doctors. Fred said their "budget was so narrow 'til we didn't have but about two-and-a-half dollars to live on for two weeks." When Patricia Ann, the couple's first child, came along in 1943, Fred decided it was time to find a job that would better support his wife and daughter.

The United States was engaged in World War II in 1943, fighting in Europe and the Pacific. Many people not directly involved in the fighting supported America's war effort by taking jobs building aircraft, ships, and munitions. Others worked at civilian jobs on army and navy bases in order to free up military personnel. Fred decided he would seek work at Brookley Air Force Base in Alabama's port city of Mobile, where he found a job driving a truck for $1.80 an hour. His days were long and sometimes busy, but many of them were spent sitting in his parked vehicle just waiting for something to do. It was during these idle moments that he began to read the Bible. Once again, he was struck with the notion of becoming a preacher.

Shortly after moving to Mobile, Fred had abandoned his Methodist upbringing, but not his faith, by joining Corinthian Baptist Church. He liked this congregation's vitality and warmth. His move to Corinthian was one that Fred considered providential, for soon he was filling in when the regular preacher was absent. He noticed that on the Sundays he preached, Corinthian's crowds were larger than usual. Fred saw this as an affirmation that he was following the path that God intended for him. His preaching style was noticed by others, too. And soon he was invited to be a substitute preacher by other churches in the area. These successes convinced him that he needed to expand his knowledge of religion. He first turned to Cedar Grove Academy, a local school set up to train black Baptist ministers. But eventually, he thought his vocational path might be improved if he studied at a better-known school. He left his job at Brookley in 1947 and set his compass for the 170-mile drive to Selma and Selma University. By this time, his family had grown to include three children: Pat, Ruby Fredericka (or "Ricky," born in 1945), and Fred Jr. (born in 1946).

At Selma, he stood out as a top student. But although he went there to prepare for a life as a preacher, he took only one course in religious studies. The remainder focused on becoming a teacher. Preaching, however, was what he liked doing best of all, and he was soon ministering to two rural churches. This was possible because each church held services just twice a month, on alternating Sundays. He added to the family income by substitute teaching.

In the fall of 1949, Fred suddenly moved his family to Montgomery so he could attend Alabama State College for Negroes to earn a teaching degree. He reasoned that teaching would provide more money than his meager ministerial income. Even so, he continued to drive the fifty miles to Selma on weekends to preach. That fall he also became a father for the fourth time with the birth of his daughter Carolyn.

By 1950, he and his family were living back in Selma, where Fred had found a regular preaching job at the First Baptist Church. This congregation was largely made up of conservative Negro professionals. Now he drove back and forth to Montgomery to attend classes, graduating in 1952 with a teaching certificate. During his two years at First Baptist, Fred's fiery, confrontational, dictatorial personality and working-class background soon soured his relationship with his more affluent, refined congregation. And at the end of 1952, he parted company with the church and returned with his family to Birmingham, where he'd grown up.

In Birmingham, Fred earned money by substitute teaching while he looked for a new church to lead. One day his friend Reverend D. L. Motley phoned him. Motley was expected to begin his ministry at Bethel Baptist Church, a black congregation in north Birmingham, the next Sunday, but he had an important program already scheduled at his current church. He asked Fred to fill in for him and preach at Bethel. Fred eagerly accepted. If the folks at Bethel liked him, perhaps they'd spread the word and another Birmingham congregation might offer him a full-time preaching job.

The next Sunday, Fred once again filled in for Motley, and the Bethel congregation liked both the man and the lively way he preached. The members invited him to become their full-time preacher. Fred declined. He didn't think it was right for church members to ask him to be their preacher when they'd already offered the job to his friend. Motley took him aside, however, and explained that he didn't really want to be Bethel's preacher. He told Fred, "'[Y]ou don't know, this may be the Lord [speaking to you]!'" Fred accepted Bethel's offer and delivered his first official sermon at the church on Sunday, March 1, 1953. He would head the church over the next eight years.

"[I]t is people in motion that make changes, not people talking, . . ."

Fred didn't start at Bethel Baptist Church thinking he'd turn it into a center for civil rights action. He just believed that his church members should be not only good Christians but also responsible citizens. When Fred started preaching at Bethel, he also became active in the National Association for the Advancement of Colored People (NAACP), an organization that fought to end racial discrimination. While most of its battles were waged in court to right injustices, the organization also encouraged Negroes to vote, as a way toward equality. As Fred explained, "[I]t is people in motion that make changes, not people talking, although it takes talk to excite people to motion." When Fred stood in his pulpit Sunday after Sunday, pressing his church members not only to register to vote but also to cast their ballots, he was taking his first steps as an actionist. As he put it, "[M]aybe your little bit [vote] could sway it [an election] one way or another." It was a challenge that was easier to talk about than it was to achieve because whites controlled the voter registration lists. They often made it difficult for blacks to register. Sometimes laws were passed requiring blacks to own property or to pay a special poll tax before their names would be added to the lists. Many Negroes in the South simply gave up trying to register to vote.

But Fred was intolerant of inaction. He had no patience for members of his church family who found it too troublesome to sign up to vote. In front of the entire congregation, he would tell individuals who had failed to register when to be dressed and ready. Then he would drive them to city hall, where he would help them with the paperwork. His religious philosophy made no distinction between a church member's spiritual needs and that member's social responsibilities. With Fred, there were no excuses for not doing what he deemed to be the right thing.

In 1954, the United States Supreme Court outlawed public school segregation in a case known as *Oliver L. Brown et al. versus the Board of Education of Topeka (Kansas)*. The *Brown* decision was named after one of thirteen parents who had filed a lawsuit against Topeka's school board because their Negro children were allowed to attend only four of the city's twenty-two elementary schools, even if a school for white children was closer to their homes. When Fred passed a newsstand after the decision was announced and saw the headlines, his heart filled with hope that it meant greater equality was just around the corner. "[I]t was almost like a new baptism of faith or a new conversion or something, that the Court had declared the segregation in schools unconstitutional." He added that it "was the biggest thing that had happened to Negroes almost since emancipation."

Yet, despite the Supreme Court decision, change did not come. "We thought that that decision itself would do a lot for attitude but it resulted in

> "although it takes talk to excite people to motion."

hardening the attitude of the Southern states." Segregation remained the social custom, especially in the South, where it often was mandated by "Jim Crow" laws. Jim Crow laws were segregation ordinances, and they covered every aspect of life in the South—separate schools, separate seating in movie houses, separate drinking fountains, separate public restrooms. But the *Brown* ruling created in Fred "a desire to push, perhaps more than usual . . . to make America what she said she was. . . ." Fred began to step out of his ministerial role at Bethel

The lives of Negroes were strictly controlled by Jim Crow ordinances that denied them full equality.

THE MURDER
of Emmett Till

Emmett Louis Till (left) was a Chicago-born Negro teenager who was visiting relatives in Money, Mississippi, in the state's Delta region, during the summer of 1955. On the evening of August 24, he went with a cousin and group of friends to Bryant's Grocery Store, where he reportedly flirted with Carolyn Bryant, a white woman. She told her husband, Roy, about it and how Emmett had whistled at her when he left the store. Roy and his half brother, J. W. Milam, decided to teach the fourteen-year-old a lesson. Taking Emmett from his relatives' house a few days later, they drove him to the Tallahatchie River, where they beat him, gouged out one eye, and then shot him in the head. They dumped his body in the river, tying a cotton-gin fan around his neck with barbed wire to weigh it down. His body was found by fishermen.

Milam and Bryant (pictured left to right with lawyer) were tried for murder, but they were acquitted by an all-white jury after only four days of testimony. Later, they confessed to the crime.

The Emmett Till murder sparked outrage in the North and became a catalyst for change in the South.

Baptist Church even more. He started to agitate for social justice. He circulated a petition among his fellow ministers that called for the immediate hiring of Negroes on the police force to patrol black neighborhoods. He and the group of ministers went to city hall on July 25, 1955, to present the petition to the commissioners. Rather than a mayor and council, Birmingham's government concentrated power in three elected officials who ran the city and individual departments within it. Commissioner James W. Morgan (who acted as mayor), Commissioner of Public Safety Robert E. Lindbergh, and Commissioner of Public Improvements Wade Bradley listened politely. The next day, they rejected the petition, saying that now was not the time to hire Negro police officers in Birmingham.

Ever persistent, Fred kept going before city leaders and pitching his request for Negro police officers. And he broadened his appeal to ask them to close bars and nightclubs that were congregated in black neighborhoods. These tended to be fraught with criminal activity. Once again, he was politely dismissed, but this time city commissioners offered a new excuse: the racial emotions stirred up by the recent murder of fourteen-year-old Emmett Till

in Mississippi on August 28, 1955, made it impossible, they claimed, for them to consider his request.

Autherine Lucy's journey to the University of Alabama began when her friend Pollie Anne Myers asked her if she wanted to apply to the school's graduate program to study library science. Lucy thought that Myers was joking, because no black student had ever been admitted. But Myers was serious. In September 1952, the two young women wrote to the university expressing their interest in attending.

The school responded by sending them application forms. A short time later, they received letters accepting them to graduate school on September 13, but when the two women arrived at the admissions office a week later and officials realized they were black, the dean of admissions turned them away, saying that a mistake had been made.

Arthur Shores, a prominent attorney, and Thurgood Marshall, head of the NAACP Legal Defense Fund and a future United States Supreme Court justice,

(*continued on next page*)

Although Fred's early efforts to integrate Birmingham's police department hadn't brought about change, he remained determined. Because of his willingness to stand up to white authority, the head of Bethel Baptist Church quickly was seen as the leader and spokesman for the city's poor and working-class Negroes. And it became more and more evident to him "[t]hat religion ought not to just be inside a church . . . it ought to challenge."

In December 1955, Rosa Parks was arrested and convicted in Montgomery, the state capital, for refusing to give up her bus seat to a standing white man. Suddenly, the atmosphere in Alabama crackled with tension as Montgomery's nearly fifty thousand Negroes organized a boycott. They were tired of Jim Crow laws that required them to sit in seats at the back of buses. They were tired of being second-class citizens. Rather than ride buses, they walked to work, took black-owned cabs, or shared rides with friends and neighbors.

Fred closely followed the news reports of the boycott. As in Montgomery, Birmingham's Jim Crow ordinances required blacks to sit in the back of buses. It was a situation that the preacher found intolerable. Fred was now the NAACP's local membership chairman. At a community-wide NAACP program, he spoke about the injustices that blacks faced and urged greater equality and opportunity. The speech brought him his first newspaper headlines, which brought him to the attention of the KKK.

heard about the women's plight and took up their cause. It was a long legal battle that saw the University of Alabama hiring private investigators to look into the backgrounds of the women. They discovered that Myers had been pregnant and unmarried at the time of her application, a fact that made her ineligible for admittance. However, the investigators could find nothing to tarnish Lucy. She decided to continue the fight without Myers.

On June 29, 1955, the U.S. District Court ruling came down in favor of Lucy. The university could not deny her admittance to the school's graduate programs on the basis of race. Two days later, the court expanded its ruling, ordering the university to drop its whites-only admissions policy.

The NAACP fought racism through the courts. In this 1956 photograph (above), Autherine Lucy is flanked by Roy Wilkins (left), NAACP executive secretary, and Thurgood Marshall, head of the NAACP's legal staff.

Not long after his NAACP speech, Fred learned that Autherine Lucy, a friend from his days at Selma University, was planning to register at the all-white University of Alabama in Tuscaloosa. It would be the first great test of the Supreme Court's 1954 *Brown* decision. On February 3, 1956, when Lucy went to enroll, Fred accompanied her and her lawyer, Arthur Shores. At first, Lucy's arrival on campus was relatively uneventful. A few white students even whispered words of encouragement to her. But on February 6, a Monday, she arrived to hostility. The Klan had used the weekend to fire up emotions of the young white college students. A crowd of between fifteen hundred and three thousand greeted Lucy by chanting, burning crosses, and hurling threats and eggs at her as she made her way from her first class to the next one. As things escalated, she was rushed to a nearby police car and, while lying on the floor, driven off campus. That evening, the university's board of trustees suspended her on grounds that it could not provide her with a safe environment—and mob violence won the day.

The Alabama Klan was not finished. Two weeks after Fred accompanied Lucy to the University of Alabama, passengers in a car threw bricks through his parsonage window. It was a warning meant to silence him. But Fred wasn't a man who yielded to threats or intimidation.

Fred continued to carry on his campaign before Birmingham's city commissioners to hire

"Negro policemen for Negro areas." Then on June 1, 1956, the state struck a blow against the NAACP, the principal organization that was winning legal ground for blacks in court case after court case. At the request of Alabama's attorney general, John Patterson, a Montgomery judge, Walter B. Jones, issued an injunction—an order—that prohibited the organization from doing business in the state because it was improperly registered. "We nicknamed him [the judge] 'Injunctionitis Jones,'" remembered Fred. He issued so many injunctions against the NAACP and the black struggle for equality that many Negroes believed white "officials could ask Jones to issue an injunction against the sunshine and . . . he would do it."

State law required businesses in Alabama to be incorporated, or registered, there. The NAACP was a New York corporation. Alabama's action was retaliation for the organization's role in the Montgomery bus boycott and Autherine Lucy's short-lived enrollment at the University of Alabama. The state court's ruling made it illegal for the NAACP to organize, conduct meetings, or perform any other business in the state. Furthermore, the order levied a fine against the organization, an attempt to bankrupt it, and required it to turn over membership lists to the attorney general. But the NAACP refused to surrender the names of its members or to pay the fine. It chose instead to fight the injunction in court.

> "We nicknamed him [the judge] 'Injunctionitis Jones.'"

The Declaration of Constitutional Principles

Through the courts, NAACP lawyers were whittling away Jim Crow ordinances. This worried most Southern lawmakers, who viewed racial segregation as a white right and way of life. They accused judges who ruled in favor of the NAACP's positions of legislating from the bench. The "Declaration of Constitutional Principles," or Southern Manifesto, was the brainchild of Senator Strom Thurmond of South Carolina, who wrote the first draft. The final draft was written by Senator Richard Russell of Georgia and read to the U.S. Senate by Senator Walter F. George, also of Georgia, on March 12, 1956. The document was a bold statement signed by 101 of the South's 128 senatorial and congressional representatives. It accused the U.S. Supreme Court of abusing its judicial power to enact law. The signers pledged to use lawful means to reverse the *Brown* decision and others that struck down segregation laws. Rather than using the South's usual arguments of black inferiority and fear of interracial marriage to justify segregation, the Southern Manifesto looked at constitutional and historical reasons to support and preserve the custom.

With the NAACP outlawed, Fred wondered what Alabama Negroes could do to stand up to white oppression. He met with Lucinda B. Robey, one of his NAACP associates and an elementary-school principal, attorney Arthur Shores, and a few others to discuss their options and the potential consequences. Shores cautioned them that any action taken on their part might result in their arrest. "[W]ell," Fred said, "somebody has to go to jail." Whatever the risks, he believed that they "must do something." To do nothing was not an option. Robey said, "'I'm . . . willing and ready to go [to jail]!'" She could have been fired for speaking so boldly against segregation, but she believed the cause of equality was more important than her job. For Fred's part, he knew in his heart "that God was not going to let . . . segregationists triumph. . . ."

They decided to call a mass meeting of Birmingham's black community at Sardis Missionary Baptist Church to decide what to do. On the Sunday before the meeting, a local minister, fearing trouble, implored Fred to call it off. Fred recalled the conversation: "[He] told me the Lord told him to tell me to call the meeting off. . . . I was in no mood to talk, and I said . . . you go back and tell the Lord, if he really wants me to call it off, he's got to come down here himself in person and tell me. . . ."

More than one thousand people crowded into the church that Tuesday night. Speaking with passion, Fred said that white leaders could outlaw

With the NAACP out of business in Alabama, Fred was named president of the Alabama Christian Movement for Human Rights, an organization set up to continue the NAACP's work in Birmingham. Beside him is Reverend Ed Gardner (right), the ACMHR vice president.

an organization, but they could not "outlaw the will of a people to be free." By the end of the meeting, they had decided to form a homegrown organization to replace the NAACP. And the person to head it? The man who had fought since his return to Birmingham to better Negro neighborhoods, challenged them to vote, and asked white city leaders to hire black police officers—Reverend Fred L. Shuttlesworth.

The Alabama Christian Movement for Human Rights (ACMHR) was born that hot June night in 1956. The new organization was formed "to challenge segregation in every form . . . [it] could." And the ACMHR started with Fred's longtime issues of voter registration and the hiring of black police officers. Fred, acting on behalf of the ACMHR, appealed to the city yet again to hire black police officers for black areas. Then, with the Montgomery bus boycott in the headlines, the organization's efforts swiftly expanded to press for the end of Jim Crow seating on Birmingham's buses.

"[S]omehow . . . ," Fred recalled, "Nelson Smith and I got wind that the Supreme Court decision on . . . [Montgomery's bus-seating ordinance] was coming down. We felt . . . it was going to be against segregation." (Reverend Nelson H. Smith, Jr., was minister of Birmingham's New Pilgrim Baptist Church, Fred's friend, and an ACMHR supporter.) "I said to Nelson . . . we don't want all the

ACMHR members signed a pledge of nonviolence in their fight for equality. Beside Fred (right, holding pledge) is Lucinda Robey.

Klansmen to be in Montgomery. . . ." So the two men devised a plan. On Thursday, December 20, when the Supreme Court's order to desegregate its buses was delivered to Montgomery, Fred sent a telegram to Birmingham's commissioners. He gave them an ultimatum: comply with the new law and desegregate Birmingham's buses by December 26 or Negroes would "rise" up if they didn't.

Christmas night, deacon Charlie Robinson and his wife called upon the Shuttlesworths. While the women and children visited in one part of the house, Fred took the deacon into a front bedroom to discuss the protest action that was planned for the next day if Birmingham's buses remained segregated. At about 9:40 p.m.— "Whoom!"—sixteen sticks of dynamite detonated outside the Shuttlesworth home, bringing down the front portion of the roof, shattering windows, and leaving much of the parsonage a smoking pile of splinters and rubble with only the Christmas-tree lights still burning. Fred had the Klan's answer to his ultimatum.

Fred and Charlie Robinson were in the front bedroom of the house when the dynamite detonated on Christmas night. Both men interpreted their survival in spiritual terms. On the left is Bethel Baptist Church.

IT IS NO SECRET WHAT GOD CAN DO!
"Underneath thee are the Everlasting arms" *Duet. 33:27*

The police said they investigated, but like so many other bombings in Birmingham, the crime was never solved. Fred knew in his gut, though, that the KKK was behind it. Here a police officer peers into the wreckage that was the front bedroom.

opposite: Fred and other unnamed ACMHR members rode the buses immediately after the Christmas Day bombing of his home and ignored the Jim Crow seating ordinance.

Amazingly, neither the Shuttlesworths nor the Robinsons were seriously hurt. Charlie Robinson came away with just a few minor cuts and commented to Fred, "'Reverend, I guess the Lord saved me 'cause I was with you.'" Fred believed his own life was spared so he could lead Birmingham's fight for justice. "[W]hen the blast went off," he said, "it wasn't intended for me to do anything but be dead. When I found I was alive I said, 'God has saved me to lead the fight and the fight is on. . . .'"

Within minutes of the blast, a crowd gathered in the street and front yard. Fred's neighbors thought that surely he must be dead. Tempers flared, with many people near the brink of violence against the few white police officers who'd responded. Fred went outside to calm them. As he made his way to the front yard, one police officer said to him, "'Reverend, I'm so sorry. . . . I know these people, . . . I didn't think they'd go this far. . . . I'll tell you what I'd do if I were you, I'd get out of town as quick as I could.'" Taking a moment to organize his thoughts, Fred responded, "Officer, you are not me. And you go back and tell your Klan brethren that if the Lord could keep me through this, and bring me out of this, tell them the war is on and I'm here for the duration, it's just beginning." And so began Fred's, and Birmingham's, long march toward racial equality.

"God has saved me to lead the fight and the fight is on...."

The very next morning, Fred called a meeting of the ACMHR. "We [are going to] do what we said we were gonna do," he announced. The day after the Klan had tried to kill him, some one hundred to two hundred people stepped forward to join Fred in defiance of the segregation ordinance. He told his followers, "[The] Klan made their history last night, we make ours for God today." They fanned out in twos and threes, so as not to tip off police of their intentions, and boarded buses all over town.

And they rode!

East. West. North. South. Some of them rode two, three, four, five times, and each time they ignored the segregation ordinance. Birmingham's Negroes became a people in motion.

The ACMHR action took the police department by surprise. City officials expected Fred to make good on his promise to defy the city's strict bus-seating ordinance. They just didn't expect him to make good on it so soon after the events of Christmas night. As a result, nobody was arrested—at least, not right away. By the time the police department figured out what was happening, the protest action was over. Later in the day, however, the police identified and arrested twenty-two people for violating the city's segregation laws.

When the case got to court, the ACMHR's attorney, Arthur Shores, argued before Judge Ralph E. Parker that seating ordinances violated the equal protection clause of the Fourteenth Amendment to the United States Constitution. The argument had been used successfully in *Brown* to overturn segregation in public schools. Parker listened, but then he convicted the riders and fined them each fifty dollars. Three days later, the judge declared the Fourteenth Amendment illegal because the federal government imposed the law on the Southern states despite their objections. (Tennessee was the only Southern state to ratify the amendment voluntarily.) But Fred and the others had ridden the buses in the first place so they could get arrested and be convicted. Now Shores could file appeals in federal court to have the convictions cleared and the law overturned—just the way it had happened in Montgomery.

In the spring of 1957, Fred continued to take action. He decided to challenge segregated seating in the waiting room at Birmingham's train depot. When he informed Ruby, she insisted on joining him despite the danger. Early in the morning of March 6, Fred alerted the media that he and his wife planned to integrate Terminal Station. An ACMHR member drove the Shuttlesworths to the depot, where a large group of angry white men waited for them at the entrance. As the crowd tried to push the Shuttlesworths away, Fred noticed a side entrance. He escorted Ruby to it, and police safeguarded their entry. After purchasing tickets, they took seats in the white waiting area and were joined by Lamar Weaver, a white man who was sympathetic to black equality and wanted to lend his support to the Shuttlesworths. They talked for a time, and then Weaver left, only to be met by the same toughs who had been waiting outside for Fred and Ruby. The thugs cursed Weaver and spewed threats and epithets. They punched him and slammed him in the face with a suitcase. Weaver made for his car with the intimidators pursuing him. Once inside his vehicle, he floored the accelerator. Although he managed to escape, he was stopped by police a short distance away and arrested for reckless driving. Appearing before Judge Parker, he was found guilty, fined twenty-five dollars, and lectured about upsetting the South's social norms.

Back at Terminal Station, Fred expected that he and Ruby would be arrested, but no arrests came. They were allowed to sit in the "whites-only" waiting area without incident. Later, Fred was surprised to learn that Birmingham had no ordinance that prohibited integrated seating at the train depot. Even so, he and Ruby had challenged the entrenched social custom of segregation.

Throughout the spring and into the summer, Fred juggled his religious responsibilities to Bethel Baptist Church with local workshops on social change through nonviolent action. He organized Monday-night mass meetings. He appeared around the country, speaking about the injustices facing blacks in the South. And he worked with the Southern Christian Leadership Conference (SCLC), the organization led by the Reverend Dr. Martin Luther King, Jr., which was set up after the Montgomery bus boycott to further desegregation. In August, Fred took another bold step when he convinced eight other families to join him in appealing to the Birmingham Board of Education to let their thirteen children attend three all-white schools. It had been three years since the Supreme Court had ruled in *Brown* that segregated schools were unconstitutional. But black children and

Ruby accompanied Fred to Terminal Station to integrate the whites-only waiting room. Both were surprised when they were allowed to wait and later board their train without arrest.

Newspapers condemned school integration as troubling and inflaming....

white children in Birmingham still attended separate schools. Of the city's eight high schools, none were integrated and three were set aside as black-only schools. Patricia and Ricky, Fred's teenage daughters, passed Phillips High School every day in order to attend Parker High School for black students. Yet Phillips was closer, and it was one of the best schools in the city. The school board promised a decision at its September 6 meeting.

While editorials in Birmingham's white-owned newspapers condemned school integration as troubling and inflaming, the Klan sent its own message to Fred. On September 2, six Klansmen snatched thirty-four-year-old Edward Judge Aaron off a street as he was walking with his girlfriend. They could have picked any black man, but the couple was alone, which made them an attractive target. Leaving his girlfriend behind, the men took Aaron to a Klan hideout, where they donned their hoods and castrated him. To intensify his pain, they doused the wound with turpentine. The turpentine actually saved Aaron's life as it cauterized the injury and kept him from bleeding to death. Deputy Tom Ellison, who made arrests in the case, said the Klansmen's "sole motive was to . . . send him [Aaron] to the Rev. F. L. Shuttlesworth . . . with a message that this would happen to any Negro sending his child to a white school."

Two of Aaron's attackers confessed and agreed to testify against their accomplices in exchange for suspended sentences. The other four pleaded not guilty, despite the testimony of their fellow Klansmen. They believed it unlikely that a jury would find them guilty because, in the South, whites usually went unpunished when the crime was against a Negro. The four Klansmen were tried separately, and the jury in each case delivered a surprising guilty verdict. Each man was sentenced to the maximum twenty years in prison. Even so, the message to blacks had been sent and received. Immediately following the public announcement of the Aaron attack, three of the eight families who had originally joined Fred withdrew their requests to enroll their children in white schools.

Fred, though, remained undeterred. At that Friday's school board meeting, no decision came. Over the weekend, he discussed the issue with his family and members of the ACMHR. He resolved that on Monday morning his family would set an example for Birmingham.

On Monday, September 9, 1957, Fred sent a telegram to city commissioners alerting them to his plans and requesting police protection. He also notified Birmingham's two television stations.

When Fred pulled up in front of Phillips High School, the television crews were there. So was a mob of angry men, who began to converge on Fred's car. Inside the car with Fred were his volunteer

ACMHR driver, Reverend J. S. Phifer; wife, Ruby; daughters Pat and Ricky; and two other children, Nathaniel Lee and Walter Wilson. Families of the two boys also had petitioned for their sons to be admitted to white schools. Seventeen-year-old Lee described the scene to a *Birmingham News* reporter: "The men attacked with brass knckles [sic] and large link chains about a foot-long and wooden [clubs]. When our car rolled up to Phillips, the men gathered around it and knocked out the windows and dented it."

In 1957, Fred attempted to enroll his daughters Pat and Ricky in all-white Phillips High School. Here the unruly group that awaited their arrival gangs up on Fred (on the right in the dark-colored shirt).

When Fred got out of the car to enter the school, fifteen to twenty men chased him, knocking him down and kicking him. Getting up, he ran in another direction until he was knocked down again. As the scene replayed over and over, four policemen who had been dispatched to the school earlier stood and watched. Fred heard one of the officers say to the attackers, "'[A]w, you don't have to do that.'" But the officer made no attempt to stop the assailants. As the assault continued, a police lieutenant tried to radio headquarters for help, but a false report of a stolen car interfered with any swift response. Coincidentally, the car reported as having been stolen belonged to segregationist and incoming police commissioner Eugene "Bull" Connor.

Fred recalled the attack: "I think they [the policemen] intended to let them get to me. . . . I know the Klansmen intended to. . . . I was struck with the brass knuckles at least twice. And kicked. . . . And my wife got out to get the girls and the young man [men] out of the back . . . and one Klansman stabbed her in the hip with a switchblade knife."

After taking several punches and blows— Fred estimated that he took at least eight to ten blows to his head—and close to losing consciousness, he realized he needed to get back to the car. A Klansman with a bicycle chain blocked his way. Somehow Fred stumbled into the man and knocked him off-balance while Phifer grabbed Fred's arms and pulled him into the car. With Fred's legs dangling dangerously out the door, Phifer raced toward the hospital.

Ruby required three stitches to close the wound to her hip.

The doctor examined and X-rayed Fred several times. He said to Fred, "'Reverend, I'm so sorry. . . . It looks like to me you had . . . a terrible beating. . . . I'm trying to find a crack in your head, at least a contusion . . . but I can't find anything. . . .'" Fred, always looking to his faith for explanation, said, "Well, doctor, the Lord knew I lived in a hard town so he gave me a hard skull." Before agreeing to release him from the hospital, the doctor advised Fred that later on he might develop problems. Dismissing the doctor's warning, Fred reasoned, "[N]o more problems than the Lord wants me to have." And he went home.

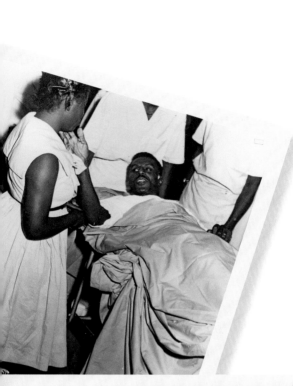

They didn't make it into Phillips High School. Indeed, they didn't make it beyond the sidewalk. In a statement released later in the day, Fred said, "[N]either official nor blood-thirsty riders [Klansmen] can stop our quest for first class citizenship. This we seek by good will, if at all possible; by law if necessary."

Despite his condition, Fred believed it was important to attend a mass meeting scheduled for that night. He knew people would have heard about the attack and that they would be angry. When he walked in, his wounds and bruises plainly visible, he told the crowd that filled the church and spilled outside, "I'm not mad and I'm not angry, 'cause I know this is what it takes for us. . . . I don't want no windowpane burst nowhere, and if anybody does [break a window] . . . I want you to report to me so I can tell the police that person did it trying to hurt the Movement." With that, Fred left the meeting early to go home to recuperate.

Three white men were arrested later for attacking and beating Fred, but they went unpunished. It was a crime against a black man— certainly not as heinous as the one committed against Edward Judge Aaron—and in the eyes of many whites, including a police department rife with Klan members or, at the very least, sympathizers, completely justifiable. Not surprisingly, the police officers who were at Phillips High School that day all claimed they were unable to identify Fred's attackers.

The Commissioner

"[W]e don't need ... out-of-towners
coming to Birmingham and agitating our people."

—EUGENE "BULL" CONNOR

KEEP...
CITY
COMMISSION
Nov. 6th

Although he professed no interest in politics. Eugene "Bull" Connor surrounded himself with powerful political allies. Photographed around 1958. he looks on as Alabama the former attorney general, greets a young fan. Commissioner James W. Morgan (1891–1971), Birmingham's acting mayor, is pictured in the white suit.

**s the newly** elected commissioner of Public Safety, Theophilus Eugene "Bull" Connor was "the law in Birmingham." He controlled the police and fire departments. In June 1958, Fred appealed to the three elected commissioners to hire black police officers as he'd done on previous occasions. Commissioner James W. Morgan said, "We will take it under advisement." Fred and his delegation of more than forty Negro ministers had heard this many times before. It was the same as hearing "No." Bull Connor was especially outraged that Fred would waste the commissioners' time with this oft-repeated plea. Bull charged that the ministers had come to the meeting only for publicity. It was his first face-to-face encounter with Fred. As few blacks dared, Fred stood his ground: "I don't think publicity is necessary and I don't want publicity. But with or without it, we intend to keep trying until we have Negroes on both the police and fire departments."

Just minutes after the meeting adjourned, Bull fumed to reporters, "I am going to instruct the chief of police to have the investigators who are working on the dynamitings [of the Shuttlesworth home] to ask Shuttlesworth to take a lie detector test . . . to clear up some rumors that have been circulating."

"I got a whole lot better acquainted with a hoe handle than I did with books...."

The Christmas 1956 bombing of Fred's home, like so many other dynamite incidents, remained unsolved, and police department officials liked to suggest publicly that the explosions had been set off by Negroes themselves to attract publicity in Northern newspapers. Such accusations deflected interest away from the police department's own affiliations with the Klan and Bull's close ties to it. Also, Bull likely thought his challenge would silence the preacher and put the Negro in his place, something he liked to brag about knowing how to do. He woefully underestimated the fiery Fred Shuttlesworth.

Theophilus **Eugene Connor** was born on July 11, 1897, in Selma, Alabama, where his father worked for the railroad. Eugene was the eldest of five children, all boys, born to Hugh King Connor and his wife, Molly. A son born before Eugene had died in infancy. Railroad families lived an almost vagabond existence during this era, and by 1905 the Connor family was residing in Atlanta, Georgia, where, when Eugene was eight, tragedy struck again. Four months after the birth of her fifth son, Mrs. Connor died of pneumonia.

Unable to care for all his children, Mr. Connor sent Eugene and his brothers to stay with relatives. Still, he spent time with them whenever he could, and Eugene traveled frequently with him as a boy.

This led Eugene to boast years later that he'd lived in thirty-six American states.

While staying with an aunt and uncle in North Birmingham, young Eugene started school. But shortly after starting, he moved to Plantersville, Alabama, to be with another aunt. Eugene remembered that in Plantersville "I got a whole lot better acquainted with a hoe handle than I did with books; I learned all about chopping cotton. . . ." Plantersville was also where "I went crazy about baseball."

In 1916, nineteen-year-old Eugene met Beara Levens, the daughter of a timber-company vice president. By this time, he'd already dropped out of school, never earning a high-school diploma, and was working as a railroad telegraph operator. A telegrapher decoded the clicks of the telegraph device. This was a skill Eugene learned from his father during their travels together. Romance blossomed between Eugene and Beara, and they were married in 1920. Shortly after the wedding, he was transferred to New Orleans, Louisiana. It was the first of many moves the couple would make while Eugene worked for the railroad. He recalled, "[M]y wife and I lived in seven different states during the first year we were married."

Eventually, Eugene embarked on a new career while living in Dallas, Texas. He combined his knowledge of telegraphy with his love of baseball and became a sportscaster. Fans unable to attend

As a telegrapher working for the railroads, Bull Connor, shown in the 1930s, lived a nomadic life until he settled in Birmingham and entered politics.

Bull's booming voice on the radio as a sports announcer earned him both a following of fans and his nickname. His popularity as a radio personality made him a shoo-in for political office.

an actual baseball game or other sporting event could go to a matinee in a downtown storefront studio where an announcer would re-create the game by using telegraphed reports that a telegrapher would decipher. Between communications, the announcer would keep the audience absorbed in the game by making up the action supposedly happening on the field. Since Eugene could decode the telegraphed accounts himself, he was able to announce each play without delays. This and his vividly imagined

Bull was a family man who wanted to pass along the traditions of the Old South to his daughter, Dora Jean, and, later, to his grandsons, Connor Frew and Eugene Vernon.

As the commissioner of Public Safety, Bull was in charge of the police and fire departments, as well as the health and education departments. A staunch segregationist, he was one of the first politicians to recognize the threat that racial accommodation posed to the ways of the Old South and vowed to firmly enforce Birmingham's segregation ordinances.

narrations made him a favorite. In 1922, he returned to Birmingham to open his own sports matinee studio. He also began working for the local radio station, where he became the voice of the Birmingham Barons, a popular minor-league baseball team. His ability to chat off-the-cuff—or "shoot the bull"— to fill dead airtime, coupled with his short stature and husky voice, earned him the nickname that would stay with him the rest of his life: "Bull." His folksy style brought him a following of fans.

On a lark, Bull ran for a seat in the Alabama House of Representatives in 1934 to see how many fans he really had. By this time, his family had grown to include a daughter, Dora Jean, born in 1928. He surprised political pundits and his opponents by winning without ever campaigning or gaining the support of a political machine. One of his most striking accomplishments during his time in the legislature was the passage of a bill to establish civil-service laws to protect state, county, and city employees. Traditionally, winning candidates fired these employees and appointed their relatives and friends to the vacancies. Now, this system of spoils was ended. He served in three sessions of the legislature. Then he resigned in 1937 to run for Birmingham's commissioner of Public Safety. Bull won this race, too. Now, he not only helped the two other commissioners make decisions about the city, but he was also in complete charge of the police and fire departments.

The young commissioner of Public Safety always seemed to be in campaign mode, courting the press and happy to share glimpses into his personal life.

Although considered a political progressive, Bull was a son of the Old South and its sharp racial divisions. Segregation was a foregone conclusion in the white-controlled South. Politicians never thought of it as a campaign issue. But as attitudes toward racial accommodation began to change at the federal level in the late 1930s and 1940s and black discontent became more evident, Bull changed his campaign message from fighting crime and lowering taxes to fighting integration. His hard line with enforcement of Birmingham's many segregation ordinances won him the support of the KKK and other white supremacist groups. He served as commissioner of Public Safety for four terms. But in 1951 his own police detectives accused him of improper conduct with his secretary, and a subsequent grand jury investigation recommended that he be fired. He decided not to seek reelection in 1953.

Then along came Fred and the ACMHR. Suddenly, the Old South and its traditions were under attack in a way Birmingham had not seen previously. Bull, itching to return to public life, had run unsuccessful campaigns for county sheriff in 1954 and commissioner of Public Improvement in 1956. In 1957, however, he seized upon the ACMHR campaign to erase Birmingham's

Police detective Henry Darnell (left) questions Bull at the Tutwiler Hotel, where Bull was discovered occupying a hotel room with his secretary, Christina Brown. In the background is hotel detective H. H. Daugherty. The resulting scandal interrupted Bull's political career.

Jim Crow ordinances in order to appeal to racists and segregationists. By only 103 votes, he squeaked back into his old job as commissioner of Public Safety. Once again, he was in charge of the police and fire departments.

After his reelection, Bull went on the offensive against the ACMHR to appease his white-supremacist constituency. While the previous commissioner of Public Safety, Robert Lindbergh, had used traffic-violation citations as a way to discourage Negroes from attending the group's mass meetings, Bull stepped up the intimidation. He assigned police detectives to attend and record the gatherings. This tactic frightened away some of the members. As head of the fire department, he dispatched trucks with lights flashing and sirens blaring to interrupt the proceedings. Sometimes fire officials, acting on Bull's orders, would declare a meeting in violation of the city's fire code, whether this was true or not, and shut it down. Bull employed these harassment tactics to squelch black efforts to end Jim Crow segregation.

But Fred had been snatched from "death's jaws" on more than one occasion—first, the Christmas-night bombing of his home, then the angry greeting he and Ruby received at the train station, and most recently his reception at Phillips High School. For him, the dream of freedom lived on. "God wouldn't let me die," he explained. In Birmingham, a Negro "couldn't be a policeman, couldn't be a fireman, couldn't drive a bus."

During his absence from public office, Bull had kept up with events so he knew Reverend Fred L. Shuttlesworth. He thought the preacher was a troublemaker.

In June 1958, Fred and a delegation of ministers went before city commissioners to make yet another appeal to hire black policemen. Polite and respectful, he presented his case. Irritated that this topic was being brought before the commissioners

He wanted
to rid
himself...
of the
pesky
preacher...
at almost
any cost.

again, Bull asserted that the ministers' actions and those of the ACMHR were hurting race relations more than helping them. Fred returned the charge. Bull became furious at the preacher's audacity and said he wouldn't vote for anything the preacher wanted. Then as soon as the meeting adjourned, and still fuming, Bull told the press that he was ordering the police department to ask Fred to take a lie detector test with regard to the unsolved Christmas-night bombing of his home in 1956. It was meant to put the Negro in his place, but Bull hadn't reckoned on Fred's confrontational nature and faith that he was doing God's work in Birmingham.

Fred returned the volley in the *Birmingham Post-Herald*. "I accept—welcome his challenge—only on these conditions: That Mr. Connor also . . . submit to a lie detector test. . . ." Among the points Fred suggested the commissioner address were the following: whether Bull was a Klansman or had Klan sympathies, whether he had ever participated in any bombings in the city, whether he knew of any police officers who had participated in any bombings in the city, and whether he personally disliked Negroes or believed them to be inferior to white people. Bull quickly let the matter drop after that, but he seethed that Fred had called his bluff in such a bold and public way. He wanted to rid himself and Birmingham of the pesky preacher from Bethel Baptist Church at almost any cost. It marked the beginning of a future filled with confrontation.

"I waited a week to see Shuttlesworth get hit with a hose. I'm sorry I missed it."

—EUGENE "BULL" CONNOR

Confro

"Mr. Conn[o]r, I say, never respected me but I respected him."

—REVEREND FRED L. SHUTTLESWORTH

ntation

Angered over Fred's refusal to quietly back down in the face of the commissioner's threats, Bull arranged for two of his police detectives to meet undercover with Jesse "J. B." Stoner Jr. (1924–2005), a leader in the Ku Klux Klan who preached hatred of blacks and Jews. Stoner eventually was found guilty of the 1958 bombing of Fred's church.

Bombings **were not** unusual in Birmingham. Since the 1940s, dynamite had been set off at more than forty black homes and churches, earning the city its nickname: "Bombingham." Like the 1956 Christmas-night blast at Fred's house that the police said they investigated, these racially motivated crimes remained unsolved.

When Fred challenged Bull to take a lie detector test about his own involvement in the bombings, it was the first time anyone from the Negro community had so boldly confronted white authority. The Klan and other radical segregationists in Birmingham who had backed Bull in the election resented that Fred still was agitating for change. Under the guise of conducting an undercover sting operation to collect evidence against bombing suspects, Bull had two of his police detectives meet with Jesse Benjamin "J. B." Stoner Jr. Stoner was a virulent white supremacist and national chairman of the National States Rights Party, the conservative political arm of the Ku Klux Klan.

Posing as steelworkers to keep their police identities hidden, the detectives met with Stoner and William Hugh Morris in Birmingham on June 21, 1958. Morris was a Klan member and an undercover police informant.

The dynamite-packed can exploded.... Shrapnel blew out windows at the church....

The detectives told the Klansmen they wanted to stop integration. Stoner said he knew some people who were good at making and detonating bombs and that they'd be willing to help for a price. Discussing several potential targets, they settled on Bethel Baptist Church because Fred was Birmingham's primary rabble-rouser. If another blast didn't scare the preacher out of town, then the detectives suggested that they would be willing to go further to eliminate him. Stoner said he knew people who could help with this, too, for slightly more money.

To protect their homes and churches from Klan violence, blacks throughout the South had begun posting armed neighborhood patrols at night. The Klan usually struck under the cover of darkness when they were least likely to be caught. In the days that followed the detectives' meeting with Stoner, Bull ordered police officers to confiscate Bethel's firearms. The policemen charged the church's watchmen with unlawful possession and took their weapons. Early the next morning, June 29, a neighbor noticed smoke rising from beside the church as she returned home from a late-night shift at work. She alerted the guards, Will Hall, a retired miner, and Colonel Stone Johnson. Johnson often acted as Fred's personal bodyguard. The two men rushed to investigate and found a five-gallon can with an ignited fuse. Acting on instinct, Hall grabbed the can and raced to the middle of the street. As soon as he set it down and ran out of harm's way, the dynamite-packed can exploded. Both guards barely escaped with their lives. Fred, shaken out of his bed in the parsonage, phoned the police and the Federal Bureau of Investigation (FBI). The crude bomb blasted a crater in the street, while shrapnel blew out windows at the church and damaged nearby homes. Flying glass injured a six-month-old baby asleep in one home and permanently scarred her face.

Birmingham police officers investigated the incident, but Bull never brought charges against anyone. The close sequence of events—Bull's embarrassment over the lie detector issue, his detectives' meeting with Stoner, and his order to remove Bethel's weapons—suggests that his real motive for the undercover operation was to get rid of Fred. No one will ever know for certain. But the 1958 Bethel Baptist Church bombing went unsolved for more than twenty years. J. B. Stoner was finally convicted of the crime in 1980 after Morris, the police informant, testified against him. Sentenced to ten years, he served three and a half years before being paroled.

Fred, believing he'd escaped death once again, now was convinced more than ever that God was providing him special protection so he could lead the fight for civil rights in Birmingham. He continued his agitation and remained the thorn in Bull's side.

But as the summer wore on, Fred soon found himself defending both his leadership of the ACMHR and his loyalty to the United States of America.

Alarmed that they were losing their way of life, Southern racists began equating any relaxation of segregation laws with Communism. Since World War II, a link to Communism brought with it unbridled fear of condemnation, potential loss of employment and friends, and accusations of disloyalty to America. Accusing people and organizations of Communist leanings was an intimidation tactic. Bull jumped on this bandwagon, hinting that Fred was a Communist and suggesting that the ACMHR and NAACP were front organizations for Communism. Citing the Cold War between the United States and its adversary, the Union of Soviet Socialist Republics (USSR), Bull said, "It is disturbing to see the Reverend Shuttlesworth starting his harassment again; with Russia [the USSR] threatening us and American soldiers exposed in foreign lands, this is a poor time for agitation at home by anyone who claims to be loyal to America." He continued, "I don't believe the Negro people of Birmingham will follow the dangerous leadership of Shuttlesworth." Finally, he speculated that Fred was "scouring the town to get 12 Negro children to leave their regular schools and try to enroll in white schools again this Fall" and also accused the minister of "raising money to build an NAACP store in Birmingham which they will use to boycott white merchants. . . ."

To the charges, Fred responded that "[t]he 'pressure, harassment and agitation' of which he [Connor] complains are necessary only because he and others in office cannot find enough good will to voluntarily speed up racial progress." He disavowed knowledge of any NAACP operation in Alabama—the organization, after all, had been outlawed in 1956—and denied that he was organizing a boycott of white merchants, which also was illegal under Alabama law. But he added, "I personally do believe . . . that in the very near future Negroes must and will begin teaching their dollars to 'have some sense' and go where they will bring equitable returns and appreciation. . . ." Never missing an opportunity to needle Bull, he reminded the commissioner that the Shuttlesworth leadership of the ACMHR had "not led to the bombing of white homes nor the castration of white persons." He promised that the pressure to hire "Negro stenographers, policemen and firemen" would continue.

As October 1958 approached, Birmingham's commissioners began to worry that the federal court was going to rule with the ACMHR in its lawsuit stemming from the December 1956 arrests for violating the bus-seating ordinance. They quickly revoked the ordinance in favor of a new one that allowed the bus company to make its own rules about seating. Unanimously approving the new ordinance, the commissioners also called for the bus company to maintain the status quo. And when the bus company announced its new policies, nothing was different. Black passengers still had to pay the driver at the front of the bus and then get off and reenter through the back door. They still had to sit in the back. The new law was simply a way of relieving the city of any direct involvement in bus segregation.

Indeed, when the decision was delivered, U.S. District Judge Harlan H. Grooms sided with the ACMHR. By then, however, the old law no longer was in effect. Fred called a special mass meeting of the ACMHR, urging his followers to violate the bus company's new policy. Bull cautioned Birmingham's blacks to ignore Fred and threatened that if they violated the bus company's seating policy, his police officers would arrest them.

But once again, the ACMHR decided to ride the buses and ignore the bus company's Jim Crow seating. Fred chose not to ride this time in order to prove to Bull that he wasn't alone in his interest in equality. Thirteen people were arrested. The ACMHR strategy had long been to fight Jim Crow segregation on several fronts at once. Fred explained it this way: "Never set a hen on one egg. Fill the nest up and some of the biddies will hatch." When the police arrived at his home to arrest him for inciting the others to violate the law, Fred was at the Western Union office sending a telegram to city commissioners demanding that they desegregate the public parks and recreational facilities. He was filling the nest. When he returned home and discovered the police had been there to arrest him, he went to city hall and surrendered. These arrests, like the

> "Never set a hen on one egg. Fill the nest up and some of the biddies will hatch."

ones before them, would be challenged in the federal court system, which was viewing segregation more and more often as unconstitutional.

More protests confronted segregation all over the country. In Greensboro, North Carolina, four black college students launched the sit-in movement on February 1, 1960, when they sat down at a lunch counter that served only whites. Ten days later, while Fred was in Greensboro to give a speech, he observed another sit-in of high-school students at the Woolworth's department-store lunch counter. These sit-ins made such an impression on the minister that he phoned the SCLC to tell Dr. King "this is a new departure and . . . we have to support these students." According to Fred, when Bull Connor heard about the Greensboro sit-ins, Bull "solemnly promised the people . . . there would be no sit-ins in Birmingham. I shot back . . . that we would have sit-ins if we wanted to." And they did.

On his return home, Fred met with students from two local black schools, Miles and Daniel Payne colleges. For maximum impact, they planned to sit in at the lunch counters of all five of Birmingham's department stores at exactly the same time. On March 31, two students entered each store and at 10:30 seated themselves at the lunch counters. Fred recalled the incident: "They sat down and they were arrested and at the jail in five minutes. . . . I didn't sit in. But I was arrested and given five convictions."

The sit-in stirred things up in Birmingham, if only briefly, and proved to Bull that local Negroes were not afraid to defy him. It also provided Fred and the ACMHR with more litigation. Subsequent sit-ins, however, fizzled when department stores simply closed their lunch counters rather than deal with protesters.

In response, Bull intensified his intimidation tactics, sending more police officers to mass meetings to take notes and jot down names. This frightened away more people, but Fred still had a contingent of followers attracted by his growing reputation and his willingness to put himself in harm's way for the sake of social justice.

During the next three years, Fred's many legal challenges against the city worked their way through the court system. The convictions for the sit-ins, and Fred's role in them, were eventually overturned—but not until the Supreme Court acted in 1963. The 1960s saw Bull fighting to keep the races apart, while Fred was shaking things up to bring about an end to Jim Crow.

In April 1960, Fred was embroiled in a libel lawsuit brought by Montgomery's police commissioner, L. B. Sullivan, and mayor, Earl D. James. Sullivan and James were suing Fred and several other ministers whose names were included in a *New York Times* advertisement sponsored by SCLC adviser Bayard Rustin and singer Harry Belafonte. The Montgomery men claimed that the advertisement subjected them, as city officials,

Many Negroes worked behind the scenes to further civil rights. Pacifist Bayard Rustin was the first to convince Reverend Dr. Martin Luther King, Jr., to lay down his weapons during the Montgomery bus boycott and to adopt a nonviolent approach to resisting white oppression based on the teachings of Mohandas K. Gandhi. He remained Dr. King's close adviser throughout Dr. King's life.

Developing a strong bond with Dr. King in the 1950s, singer Harry Belafonte mobilized other artists, black and white, to support the civil rights movement. Using their celebrity status but usually working quietly, Belafonte, singer and actor Lena Horne, and others in the film and recording industries raised money to help those on the front lines of advancing equality of opportunity.

to ridicule and embarrassment for the police department's efforts to squelch student protests in February, and they sought $500,000 in damages from each defendant. The full-page ad described the students' expulsions after truckloads of shotgun-toting police surrounded Alabama State College campus. By the end of May, Governor John Patterson, the former attorney general, filed a similar suit on behalf of the state of Alabama. Fred also was named as codefendant, along with *The New York Times* and its reporter Harrison E. Salisbury, in a lawsuit launched by Bull over an article called "Fear and Hatred Grip Birmingham." The article characterized Bull as having made his political comeback on a platform of racial hatred and quoted him as saying, "Damn the law—down here we make our own law."

In the Sullivan case, the state courts agreed with the plaintiffs. As soon as the decision was announced, sheriffs confiscated the automobiles belonging to Fred and the other ministers and auctioned them off to pay a portion of the judgment against them. Later, the U.S. Supreme Court reversed the lower court's decision, and the state of Alabama eventually returned to Fred and the other ministers the money it had received for the vehicles. The Supreme Court's Sullivan ruling became an important precedent to later free speech cases. Bull's case dragged on and on but finally, in 1966, the U.S. Court of Appeals, citing the Sullivan decision, ruled that Bull had failed to show libel on the part of any of the defendants.

It was 1961, and Birmingham remained a city ruled by Jim Crow and Bull Connor. Blacks and whites still attended separate schools. They ate in separate restaurants. They went to separate churches. They drank water from separate fountains. Blacks could enter white-owned department stores to spend their money, but they were not welcome to use the dressing rooms or bathrooms reserved for whites. And blacks still were not represented on the police force. In a landslide victory, Bull was reelected commissioner of Public Safety. He attributed this

In Birmingham, one of the most segregated cities in the country, Jim Crow reigned, creating parallel services within the larger community. Negroes were relegated to sit in the balconies of theaters, attended their own churches, and rode in "Colored Only" cabs, while whites got the choicest theater seats and had their own churches and cab companies.

COLORED ONLY

COUNTRY'S CABS   PHO

THE CONGRESS OF RACIAL EQUALITY

The roots of the Congress of Racial Equality (CORE) stretch back to the 1940s and the Fellowship of Reconciliation (FOR), a pacifist organization. Originally called the Committee of Racial Equality, it was founded by FOR members in 1942 to end inequality between whites and blacks in the United States through the philosophy of nonviolent resistance taught by Mohandas K. Gandhi. In 1947, CORE sponsored the first interracial Freedom Ride—the Journey of Reconciliation—when several pairs of white and black men tested the Supreme Court's ban on segregated bus seating in interstate travel by journeying into the South. The early Freedom Riders gained national attention when four of them—two Negroes and two whites—were arrested in Chapel Hill, North Carolina, for violating local segregation laws and sentenced to work on a chain gang. Interestingly, the judge in the case initially sentenced the two whites to longer terms than the black men because he thought it would teach liberal white Northerners a lesson about interfering in the ways of the South. The Freedom Rides of the 1960s were modeled after the 1947 Journey of Reconciliation.

success to his hard stance on segregation, and many blacks believed that equality would be a long time coming to Birmingham. But other people thought they could speed the process of integration.

On May 4, seven black and six white members of the Congress of Racial Equality (CORE) boarded two buses in Washington, D.C., bound for New Orleans in the first Freedom Ride. These Freedom Riders had but one purpose: to speed integration by dramatizing the disparity between federal law and local reality. Since the late 1940s, segregation on buses and trains that crossed state lines had been illegal. Yet it was still practiced in most of the South. And Negroes who challenged this custom were arrested.

Riding together in racially mixed pairs on the buses and sharing their meals in bus terminals as they made their journey, the riders encountered only minor hostilities along the way. Their route took them through Virginia, North and South Carolina, and Georgia before heading west toward New Orleans, where they were scheduled to arrive on May 17. When they crossed from Georgia into Alabama, events took an abrupt turn.

James Peck, one of the riders, phoned Fred before church services on Sunday morning, May 14—Mother's Day—and told him the time they expected to arrive in Birmingham that afternoon. Having heard rumors that the Klan was planning a reception for the outsiders and knowing what its members were capable of, Fred warned Peck to be careful and

NEWSLETTER

AUGUST, 1961
BIRMINGHAM, ALABAMA

"THE MAN FOR BIRMINGHAM"

REV. F. L. SHUTTLESWORTH

Rev. Shuttlesworth is hailed by CBS Reporters as "The man most feared by Southern Racists, and the voice of the new militancy among Birmingham Negroes". Bombed twice, and beaten by mobsters, he is currently involved in 27 criminal and civil actions; seven of which came as a result of the Freedom Rides. He has been jailed about 8 times—four times during the Freedom Rides!

He has sentences totaling about 3½ years in time, and $5,000.00 fines. He is sued for $3,000,000 in the Times Suits, and with three other Negro Alabama Ministers has lost a car and property.

Mrs. Shuttlesworth, once stabbed in the hip during a mob, has developed a nervous stomach condition. The three older children were arrested in Gadsden and convicted on "Delinquency" charges in August-Sept., 1960, and are now under bond. His drivers license has been suspended for a whole year.

Rev. Shuttlesworth is determined to see the Birmingham struggle end in victory. Although he has accepted Pastorate of a Cincinnati Church, he will, at the unanimous request of the Movement continue to be its leader, commuting weekly, or as often as necessary to insure positive leadership.

At the requests of his other Civil Rights Compatriots, he will continue to be Secretary of the Southern Christian Leadership Conference, Atlanta, Georgia, and a Board Member of the Southern Conference Educational Fund, New Orleans, La. So the South has not finished with Shuttlesworth, — nor has Shuttlesworth finished with the South.

"LET EVERY MAN REMEMBER THAT TO VIOLATE THE LAW IS TO TRAMPLE ON THE BLOOD OF HIS FATHER, AND TO TEAR THAT CHARTER OF HIS OWN CHILDREN'S LIBERTY".

—ABRAHAM LINCOLN

OBJECT OF FREEDOM RIDES

By W. E. Shortridge,
ACMHR Treasurer

We, in Birmingham, more or less, inherited the Freedom Rides. The plans for the rides originated in Washington, D. C., as most of us are aware of by this time. CORE seems to have initiated the idea. Our participation was due to force of circumstances. We have been prone to cooperate with any force which has for its purpose the breaking down of Freedom Barriers. Consequently, everyone concerned looked to us for guidance, advice, assistance and cooperation. Knowing what we stand for and have pledged to do, we had to get into the act or the situations would have been much worse from a violent standpoint.

We realize that to change or make a decided improvement in laws and customs of a local nature which is in conflict with federal laws, it is necessary to demonstrate to the world what is actually happening in the South and especially in Birmingham. Therefore, we approved the Freedom Rides whole-heartedly. Federal laws have been flagrantly violatd to the distate of traveling citizens. To implement federal laws and let the world know what Negroes are subjected to, it seems it was necessary to go right into a demonstration of these inhuman atrocities by subjecting ourselves to inhuman treatments. We got it alright, and, as results, in thirty days all signs at Bus and Train stations designating "White and Colored" have been removed.

Had not such demonstrations been put on, those signs would have remained indefinitely.

SEGREGATION IS A SIN— A CANCER

Telling Negroes that they are not ready to integrate into the total American stream, is like saying it is wrong for a man to beat his wife, but she is not ready for him to stop.

I am willing to say this the world over, the problem is not in Education, Economic strength, nor Racial Conduct; it is based 98% on color.

Now, if Negroes were segregated and discriminated because they were not educated, then we could go to school. If Negroes were segregated and discriminated because of their economic strength, then perhaps each Negro would see to it that he had enough money. If it is racial conduct, then we would improve our conduct. But the sin is, that we are segregated and discriminated where we can't do anything about it. IT IS MOSTLY THE COLOR. This is a SIN against GOD and MAN. SEGREGATION MUST DIE . . . IF AMERICA IS TO LIVE!

They sabotaged the bus by cutting its tires and ... swarmed around it and set it afire.

to expect trouble when they arrived. Hanging up, he sent word to Bull and Jamie Moore, the police chief, advising them of the riders' schedule and requesting protection for them. Later, during his sermon, he prayed with his congregation for the travelers' safe journey. Their journey was anything but safe.

In Anniston, Alabama, an angry mob met one bus. After failing to oust the riders, they sabotaged the bus by cutting its tires and then followed it until it became disabled. Once the bus stopped, they swarmed around it and set it afire. As the travelers emerged, choking and coughing, the gang beat them with chains, pipes, clubs, and fists until a law officer scared them away by firing his pistol.

Meanwhile, when the other bus reached Anniston an hour after the first one had been set afire, Klan thugs boarded it and began beating the Negroes sitting in the front seats. They bodily moved them to the rear of the bus and stood guard over them for the two-hour ride to Birmingham.

When the bus pulled into the Birmingham station, some twenty-five whites were waiting for it. They carried with them razor-sharp chains, metal pipes, and clubs. The attackers rushed the bus and began pummeling the riders. As the melee unfolded, it spilled into an alley, where James Peck was beaten unconscious.

Fifteen minutes after the attack began, the Birmingham police showed up. By then, the assault was over and the segregationists, gone.

It was rumored that Bull had ordered the police to delay their response to give the Klan time alone with the riders. He denied the charge at the time, but years later a message from the local FBI office to Director J. Edgar Hoover was discovered that indicated Connor had said he wanted the Freedom Riders beaten until it looked as if they'd been attacked by bulldogs. The memo also revealed that the police department had promised to delay its response by fifteen minutes to give the Klan time to do its work.

Upon regaining consciousness sometime after being attacked, Peck managed to find a taxi driver who was willing to take him to Fred's house. Then other victims began to show up, too. Hearing about the incident in Anniston and despite the danger, Fred organized an ACMHR caravan to collect the injured riders there and shuttle them back to the safety of his house. Once again, Fred was in violation

left: **James Peck (1914–1993), a CORE official, rode into Birmingham with Freedom Riders and was beaten unconscious by KKK members. Here he speaks at a press conference about his ordeal.**

right: **Fred was a target not only of the KKK but also of Commissioner of Public Safety Bull Connor. Fred worked to find a way to get the Freedom Riders safely out of Birmingham but was booked into jail for his efforts.**

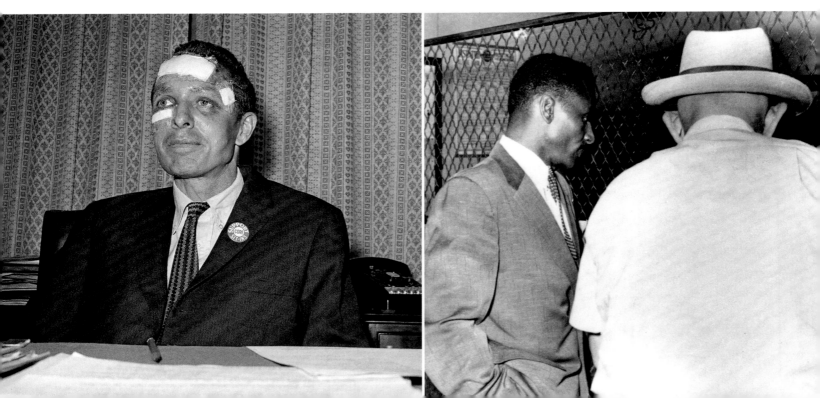

of the law by breaking local residential segregation ordinances that prohibited blacks and whites from being housed together. Bull threatened to arrest him—but it was mere harassment.

Fred phoned Robert F. Kennedy, the attorney general of the United States, several times to discuss how to evacuate the riders from the city. He also called Governor Patterson, who promised to escort them only to the nearest Alabama state line. They'd be on their own after that.

Unable to find any willing bus drivers to take them to New Orleans, the Freedom Riders decided that their goal had been accomplished. They had received national and international publicity highlighting the reality of racism in the South. Indeed, photographs of the Freedom Ride attacks appeared in newspapers around the world and embarrassed a group of local business leaders who happened to be in Tokyo to promote commerce with Birmingham.

The next fall, after an intense investigation by the FBI, six defendants were brought to trial in federal court for the Anniston bus burning. The jury failed to reach a decision and a mistrial was declared, but Judge Grooms ordered a retrial. At first, the men entered pleas of not guilty. Later, they changed their pleas to no contest and were found guilty. Judge Grooms placed five of the men on probation. The sixth man, a nineteen-year-old who was already serving a ten-year sentence for a burglary committed after the Anniston bus attack, was sentenced to an additional year and one day in prison. All were ordered to sever their ties to the KKK.

The first Freedom Ride might have ended when the riders boarded a plane out of Birmingham. But young college students from Nashville, Tennessee, decided they would pick up where the first wave of riders left off. And when they arrived in Birmingham, Fred was there for them, too. In this Southern city, he *was* the civil rights movement.

Yet, even as Howard K. Smith, a reporter for CBS television news, called Fred the man that Southern segregationists feared more than any other, some of his ACMHR cohorts wondered just how strong his commitment to Birmingham was. They were aware that Revelation Missionary Baptist Church had asked him to come to Cincinnati, Ohio, to become its preacher. Revelation members had offered the job to Fred because they wanted

Fred talks with a racially mixed group of Freedom Riders in the whites-only waiting room of the bus station. Mary McCollum (right), a student in Nashville, Tennessee, was one of two white students identified in this wave of integrationists. All were later detained by the police.

someone well known and with distinction to lead their church. Ruby, although committed to civil rights, was ready to put Birmingham behind her. She worried about her children and their ability ever to find jobs in a city where the name *Shuttlesworth* would likely generate roadblocks. It concerned her that they had to live where her husband and their father was the subject of a firestorm of media criticism and where telephone threats were an almost daily occurrence.

Fred's sweat and blood had spilled on Birmingham's soil; he was part of the city, and it was part of him.

Throughout the spring of 1961, Fred weighed Revelation's offer. On the one hand, he believed that his work in Birmingham was unfinished. On the other, Cincinnati would be better for his family, and he would make more money. In the end, family and finances won out. On June 2, he announced his decision to accept Revelation's offer. If Bull thought that he was finally rid of the minister, he was soon to get a wake-up call. Fred's sweat and blood had spilled on Birmingham's soil; he was part of the city, and it was part of him. Hadn't God saved his life time and again so he could lead its struggle for equality and justice? Fred reasoned that he could

Fred ...
could live in
Cincinnati
and ...
still work
to "dehorn"
Bull.

live in Cincinnati and still continue his work in Birmingham. He could still work to "dehorn" Bull. And that's what he did.

He moved to Cincinnati in August 1961 but made the four-hundred-mile trip to Birmingham every other week or so to plan strategies with the ACMHR. As far back as 1958, Fred had asked the commissioners to desegregate the public parks, golf courses, and swimming pools, and they had not done so. So Fred had sued to desegregate them. The same month that Fred took up residence in Cincinnati, Judge Grooms ordered Birmingham's recreational venues desegregated by January 15, 1962. Bull appealed the decision, but lost. So he convinced the two other commissioners to close these facilities rather than integrate them. Bull feared that if the parks were desegregated, the schools would follow, and he would have none of that. But it was a move that hurt both blacks and whites. It angered everyone. Business leaders who already were embarrassed by the worldwide notoriety heaped on Birmingham following the KKK's attack on the Freedom Riders were especially offended by Bull's latest maneuver.

Black professionals quickly organized to negotiate with white business leaders over the parks issue. They squeezed Fred out of these negotiations, using the pretext that he was no longer a Birmingham resident. In truth, white business leaders didn't wish to legitimize Fred's claims to leadership by meeting with him—even if they

Bull announced that he was running for governor of Alabama.

disagreed with Bull and were thinking it was time for him to go—while black professionals were mainly uneasy with Fred's confrontational, dictatorial style. Many of Fred's ACMHR followers believed he was being slighted, and they resented it. Mostly poor or working class, his loyalists viewed the black professionals as newcomers to the struggle for equality because they had not challenged Jim Crow the way the ACMHR had.

As the groups negotiated, the new year brought with it bomb blasts at three more black churches on January 16. None of these churches had participated in the ACMHR mass meetings, but the violence occurred the day that Judge Grooms sentenced the six defendants for the Anniston bus burning. Shortly before this, Bull announced that he was running for governor of Alabama. And by the end of the month, Fred began serving a ninety-day sentence in Birmingham's jail, having lost his appeal to overturn the 1958 conviction for inciting ACMHR members to violate the city's bus-seating ordinance. Not content to idle away time in his cell, he needled the commissioners by sending them a petition asking for the desegregation of courthouse facilities. His petition brought about no changes, of course, but it was an irritant to the commissioners, which was something of a victory. He served just thirty-six days of his sentence before Judge Grooms ordered his release, citing that the conviction was based on an unconstitutional ordinance.

Once out of jail, Fred started making more plans for Birmingham—and thinking about other ways to inflame Bull Connor.

He requested that white merchants hire Negro sales clerks. Once again, the merchants wouldn't discuss it with him. But that didn't stop Fred. He worked with Miles College activists and their student-body president, Frank Dukes, a Korean War veteran, to apply pressure. Meeting with white merchants several times in February 1962, the students privately kept Fred abreast of discussions and were taking their lead from him. When these talks produced no results, the students, with Fred's full support, began a selective-buying campaign—since boycotts were illegal—urging blacks to wear their old clothes or buy their Easter wardrobes only from stores that hired black clerks.

Soon, merchants were feeling an economic pinch. They went to city commissioners and asked if they could integrate their sales forces. Bull threatened to arrest any that violated the segregation ordinances. And in retaliation, he vowed to cut off a program that provided food to poor families, most of whom were black.

When Fred went downtown one day to see how the selective-buying campaign was going, he was arrested for blocking the sidewalk. He was fined yet again and sentenced to sixty-one more days in jail. Like his other sentences, this one eventually was quashed by the federal courts, but not for years to come. Although the selective-buying campaign couldn't and didn't last forever, it proved to the black community that it could bring economic pressure to bear on the powerful white elite.

Bull's run for governor was short-circuited when Judge George C. Wallace, who vowed to stand up to federal laws forcing school desegregation, was selected to run on the Democratic ticket against a weak Republican candidate. As the governor's race moved into high gear in May 1962, some of Birmingham's more moderate white leaders looked

Although both Bull Connor and Judge George C. Wallace had strong credentials as segregationists, Wallace won the nomination for governor on the Democratic ticket. Blacks, however, protested his nomination.

for a way to nudge Bull out of office. They called for a change in city government from its current commission form to a mayor-council structure in which the mayor would be elected directly by the voters. The group thought this change would be better for Birmingham because power would be more dispersed and it would offer more checks and balances. Getting wind of the push for a new city government, Bull fell back on a familiar charge. He claimed that the people calling for the change were Communists.

Birmingham's political and social structure was soon to face other challenges. Ever since the SCLC was formed in 1957, Fred had been after Martin Luther King, Jr., to bring the organization to Birmingham. He believed that if this city, one of the most racially segregated in America, could be desegregated, the rest of the nation would follow. He was certain the SCLC's presence would shine the national spotlight on racial conditions there and help bring about change. In May 1962, Dr. King finally announced that his organization would hold its annual convention in Birmingham in September. Fred was excited by the prospect of hosting the SCLC. But the white merchants who wanted to oust Bull worried that if there were demonstrations or Klan violence while Dr. King was in town, people would vote to keep Bull in charge. The group's leader, Chamber of Commerce President Sidney Smyer, telephoned A. G. Gaston, a millionaire and Birmingham's most prominent black businessman,

"'I got the money but Fred got the people. . . .'"

A. G. Gaston (1892–1996) sometimes was criticized for not taking a more visible role in the fight for equality. But like many other prominent blacks, he often worked behind the scenes, sometimes providing bail money for arrested protesters or paying their legal expenses.

for help. As Fred reported it, Gaston told Smyer, "'I got the money but Fred got the people. . . . [Y]ou have to talk to him.'" The "people" Gaston was speaking of were Fred's ACMHR soldiers, the ones most likely to protest.

When Fred met with Smyer and several downtown merchants, Smyer asked him to avoid staging marches or demonstrations while Dr. King was in town. He tried to get on Fred's good side by calling him "doctor," but Fred wasn't someone who could be wooed by flattery. So he told Smyer and the others, "[N]o, there is no other alternative to demonstration if y'all don't do something." He was bargaining for integration. Then, in a gutsy move, he announced, "I have decided that Martin Luther King, Ralph [Abernathy] and I are going to be arrested at your store. . . . [A]nd when we come out [of jail] looking bad [unkempt], folks won't go to your store." (Reverend Ralph Abernathy was an SCLC adviser to Dr. King and his right-hand man.) Hearing Fred's threat, one of the merchants excused himself on the pretext of making a phone call. When he returned, he explained that a painter accidentally put paint over one of the Colored Only signs in his store, and the merchant liked it so much that he was thinking about having him paint over all the other signs in his store if Fred would agree not to march. Fred grinned, thinking it was a start, and said, "[N]ow you are a wise thinking White man. If all of you were like that we wouldn't have these problems."

The other merchants fell in line, agreeing to remove or paint over the segregation signs. As agreed, Fred made no public announcement of his arrangement with the businessmen, but he warned them that if the signs returned—and he expected them to—the fight would resume. In late September, Dr. King and the SCLC held their meeting without demonstrations. Birmingham was quiet.

"[S]egregation today... segregation tomorrow... segregation forever."

Then in early October, after Dr. King and the SCLC left town, Bull sent inspectors to all of the department stores. He ordered the Jim Crow signs replaced, threatening to arrest owners and close their stores if they failed to do it. For Birmingham's Negroes, it had been a short-lived victory. Fred, though, was true to his word. The fight resumed as 1962 drew to a close. The ACMHR and the SCLC planned for major joint demonstrations in the spring.

The November elections ushered in a new governor, George C. Wallace, who vowed in his January 14, 1963, inaugural speech, "[S]egregation today... segregation tomorrow... segregation forever." And shortly after the election, segregationists bombed Bethel Baptist Church for the third time, on

George C. Wallace (1919–1998) eventually would serve four terms as Alabama governor and also would run for the presidency of the United States four times. He was adamantly opposed to the federal government's role in school desegregation and thought individual states should be able to decide the issue for themselves, even if blacks often were denied the opportunity to express an opinion.

As Birmingham debated a new form of government, Bull often appeared in community forums to express his opposition to it.

December 14. The bombers struck using the same method as in 1958—a five-gallon can full of dynamite. This blast, like the one before it, rained shrapnel in a wide swath, blew out the church's windows, and damaged the preacher's house next door.

In Birmingham, the people voted to change their form of government. A special March 5 election was scheduled to choose a mayor. In the meantime, the commissioners would continue to run the city. Albert Boutwell, the former lieutenant governor of Alabama, announced his intention to mount a campaign for the office. Bull declared that he would run against Boutwell. Of the two men, Boutwell was considered more moderate on racial issues, but he was still a segregationist.

Some Negroes hoped that a Boutwell victory would make the demonstrations unnecessary. But Fred disagreed. He lobbied to set an early date for the protest marches because he was almost certain Bull would do something that would help the cause of civil rights.

On March 5, Boutwell and Bull came in first and second in a four-way mayoral contest, so a runoff election was scheduled for April 2 between the two men. When the votes in the April 2 election were tallied, Boutwell was the winner and Birmingham's new mayor. The only hitch was that Bull and the

two other commissioners refused to give up their jobs until their terms expired in 1965. They sued to prevent Boutwell from taking office. But he took office anyway, and for a while Birmingham had two competing governments.

The previous fall, the SCLC had sent Wyatt Tee Walker, Dr. King's chief of staff, to Birmingham to help Fred plan the joint ACMHR-SCLC spring demonstrations. Walker agreed with Fred that the time to protest was while Bull was still in power. He gave the demonstrations a code name: "Project C." The *C* was for "confrontation."

Project C was put into play on April 3, 1963, one day after the runoff election, and Birmingham suddenly became the nation's focus of attention.

Fred sent two ACMHR members, Lola Hendricks and Reverend Ambus Hill, to city hall to get a parade permit. Birmingham law required that people have a permit in order to march in the streets and that's what the ACMHR and SCLC planned to do. Bull denied the permit and told the two that he'd march them into jail if they didn't get out of city hall.

A few blocks from city hall, Fred was passing out copies of the "Birmingham Manifesto" to passersby. A leaflet written by Walker but with Fred's name on it, the manifesto announced the onset of peaceful demonstrations and demanded the immediate desegregation of lunch counters, restrooms, and drinking fountains in downtown department stores;

opposite: **In April 1963, Project C got underway. Here an unnamed woman is stopped and cited by police officers for demonstrating against the unfair hiring and service practices of Birmingham's department stores.**

Blind singer Al Hibbler (1915–2001), originally from Mississippi, joined in the Birmingham protests and was confronted by Bull.

opposite: An unnamed Negro protests on the sidewalk in front of Loveman's Department Store: "Jim Crow Must Go."

ENTRANCE
STORE for MEN
WE'LL BUY
WHEN LOVEMAN'S
HIRES
NEGRO CLERKS
JIM CROW
MUST GO.

fair hiring practices in Birmingham businesses; dismissal of charges against ACMHR members for their previous protests; the reopening of recreational facilities on an integrated basis; and the establishment of a biracial committee to work out a schedule for desegregation in other areas of life. It also called on all citizens—black and white—to help shape Birmingham's destiny by joining the protests.

Later in the day, as Fred spoke to reporters, college students and others who had been recruited at a mass meeting the evening before simultaneously staged the first Project C demonstration. Numbering about two dozen, the volunteers converged on four downtown department-store lunch counters and quietly waited to be served—or arrested. Since the Jim Crow signs had been put back following Bull's October order, the protesters had no real hope of being served. Instead, the police arrested them, and Bull provided them with accommodations in Birmingham's jail. This quiet demonstration and the arrests inspired others to attend a mass meeting scheduled for that night and to get involved.

The next day, another round of sit-ins fizzled when the same four department stores closed their lunch counters. The fifth department store posted a thug at the entrance to discourage protesters. Although only four more arrests were made, Bull vowed that as long as he had an office at city hall he would fill the jails before he'd yield to segregation.

> But how long were Negroes to wait for equality?

It already
had been
one hundred
years since ...
Lincoln
signed the
Emancipation
Proclamation
... and still
they were ...
not truly free.

Not everyone endorsed the demonstrations. Middle- and professional-class blacks agreed with the goals of the movement but largely disapproved of the methods and timing. Many resented Fred's heavy-handed style. They declined to speak out publicly against either Fred or Dr. King, but they worried about their livelihoods and preferred a more patient course. They assumed that eventually equality would come.

White people in Birmingham weren't of one mind either. Although some wished to see an end to segregation, their voices—if they spoke out at all—were drowned out by others adamantly opposed to integration and more vocal, like Bull Connor and the Klan. It seemed that everyone was opposed to the timing of the demonstrations. Mayor Boutwell called Fred and Dr. King outside agitators because neither resided in Birmingham, and accused them of being there only to stir up trouble and get publicity. A major broadside came when Father Albert Foley, a Jesuit priest who was chairman of the Alabama Advisory Committee to the U.S. Commission on Civil Rights, called the demonstrations poorly timed.

But how long were Negroes to wait for equality? How patient should they be? When *was* the right time to voice discontent with injustice? It already had been one hundred years since President Abraham Lincoln signed the Emancipation Proclamation in 1863 and still they were not free—not truly free. They could not drink from the same water fountains

After the lunch counter sit-ins fizzled, Fred (front right) volunteered to lead a march. A small group joined him, but Bull and Police Chief Jamie Moore stopped them a short distance away from where they began. Rather than turn around, as ordered, they knelt in prayer. Bull ordered Moore to arrest them.

as whites or go for a summer swim in whites-only public pools. Their education was limited to schools set aside for black students, even when schools for white students were more convenient and better equipped. And, in Birmingham, the view from the back of the bus still revealed no black police officers. No, they were not free.

Fred and Walker realized that lunch counter sit-ins were too easily thwarted. A bolder approach was needed to generate larger protests. Fred volunteered to lead a march from the Sixteenth Street Baptist Church. His arrest was certain to ignite a spark.

On April 6, after reminding his fellow marchers about the methods of nonviolent direct action, he and forty-two ACMHR-SCLC protesters filed out of the church and walked two-by-two across Kelly Ingram Park— the line of demarcation between black and white Birmingham. After the group walked three blocks, and with Bull looking on, Police Chief Jamie Moore stopped them in front of the federal building and ordered them to turn back. They were parading without a permit. Instead of turning back, though, Fred directed his followers to kneel with him in prayer. As they prayed, Bull gave the arrest order, and they were taken away to jail.

The next day—Palm Sunday—John T. Porter and Nelson H. Smith, Jr., joined Alfred D. King, Dr. King's brother, in leading another march. All three were preachers at local churches.

Spectators gathered along the route to cheer on the ministers. This time trouble erupted when the spectators became angry over a new police tactic: the use of dogs to quell the protests. Unlike the marchers, the spectators were untrained in nonviolent resistance. One young man reportedly lashed out at a dog with a sharp clay pipe. When the dog responded and pinned the young man to the ground, bystanders rushed to his aid. This drew more police with dogs. By the time police suppressed the crowd, they had arrested and taken into custody another twenty-six marchers and onlookers.

The Palm Sunday protest achieved something the previous one did not. Photographs that showed Bull's police dogs attacking the young man appeared in newspapers around the globe. These helped confirm conditions under which Negroes lived in the South. The images also embarrassed and worried downtown business leaders. They had barely survived the selective-buying campaign the previous Easter. Would shoppers shun downtown stores again because of the demonstrations?

Bull ordered trained German shepherds to help his police officers quash the spring 1963 protests, but their use backfired on the commissioner and brought unwanted negative publicity for Birmingham.

When Fred was released from jail the day after Palm Sunday, he learned that the city sought an injunction against the movement leaders—Dr. King, Ralph Abernathy, and himself. Later that Monday evening, a judge signed the order. It prohibited the leaders from marching. If they continued to lead demonstrations, they would be arrested. The next day, after receiving legal council and discussing it with Fred, Dr. King announced that they would defy the order and the protests would continue.

On Good Friday, April 12, Dr. King, Abernathy, and Fred led some fifty or so marchers out of the Sixteenth Street Baptist Church. Another five hundred to one thousand onlookers fell in step behind them as they proceeded toward the downtown

(From left to right): Fred, Reverend Ralph Abernathy (1926–1990), and Reverend Dr. Martin Luther King, Jr. (1929–1968), led the Palm Sunday march wearing blue jeans instead of their usual business suits to represent their stand with everyday working folk. Fred, however, quipped that they were wearing them so the city wouldn't need to provide workclothes when they were arrested. And arrested they were.

When Bull
gave the order
to arrest
the leaders,
Dr. King and
Abernathy
knelt in prayer.

business district a few blocks away. Along the way, Fred withdrew from the march. It was important to avoid having all three leaders in jail at the same time.

As the marchers made their way downtown, they were met by a large contingent of police. When Bull gave the order to arrest the leaders, Dr. King and Abernathy knelt in prayer. The police officers seized them and shoved them inside waiting paddy wagons. The demonstrators who were marching with them also were arrested, along with many onlookers, who shouted, sang, and taunted police. Before the march, Dr. King and the others had decided he would remain in jail rather than post bail. They thought his confinement would create publicity that would lead to bigger protests all around the country. They also hoped it would inspire people to send donations to help other marchers pay their bail amounts.

The police visited Fred later that day and told him they had photographs that showed him participating in the march. They arrested him, but he promptly paid his bail and was released.

Dr. King, however, remained in jail for eight days. During his confinement, the protests continued, including an attempt to desegregate white churches on Easter Sunday. As arrests mounted and jail cells filled, eight white clergymen published an appeal to Dr. King in the local white-owned newspaper. Their open letter called the protests "unwise and untimely" and urged the local Negro community to withdraw its support of the demonstrations. When Dr. King read their statement, he responded, in the margins of the newspaper, with his "Letter from Birmingham Jail," in which he explained why people must disobey unjust laws. He told the clergymen that they and others like them who urged a more patient course were responsible for blacks' continued second-class treatment.

Meanwhile, Fred worked to keep the bail contributions flowing and the demonstrations going. Dr. King was released from jail on April 20, and by the end of the month the protests began to wane as people worried about the repercussions of participating in them, or simply lost interest. The leaders knew they had to create an approach that would reignite people's emotions—or they might lose Birmingham to Bull Connor and the status quo.

James Bevel, the SCLC's twenty-six-year-old director of Direct Action and Nonviolent Education, came up with the idea to mobilize children in the protests. Fred immediately warmed to the concept. Children were free of responsibilities and were enthusiastic. Wyatt Walker agreed. But when the trio took the idea to Dr. King, he worried. How would it look if the children were injured? What would people think? Would using children hurt the movement? While Dr. King deliberated—always examining things thoroughly and considering consequences— Fred was more inclined to act. He pushed for the idea.

Reverend James Bevel's youth attracted a strong following among Birmingham's young people. Bevel (1936–2008) came up with the idea to use children in the Project C demonstrations and coordinated their participation through workshops on nonviolent direct action.

The black elite were appalled that the leaders would consider enlisting their children to march. They steadfastly opposed the idea. Many of their children, though, were tired of seeing their parents cower in the face of white oppression.

Bevel recruited influential teens and church youth-group leaders to attend his workshops on nonviolent direct action at the Sixteenth Street Baptist Church. It was one of the largest churches in Birmingham and close to the downtown business district and city hall. These youths, in turn, brought their friends. Fred was a fixture at the training sessions and regaled the young people with tales of

> Officers roared back and forth in ... a tank on wheels— and tried to corral the kids.

his past brushes with the Klan—and with Bull. He strategized with them. In return, they admired his faith that he was doing the Lord's work. They were inspired by his bravery—and determination. And they were ready to take to the streets in the name of freedom.

The children's march began on May 2 when Bevel arranged for two radio disc jockeys to announce that there was going to be a party in the park and that kids should bring their toothbrushes. It was a message in code. It meant that there was going to be a demonstration in Kelly Ingram Park, which lay diagonally across the street from the Sixteenth Street Baptist Church, and that kids should come prepared to spend the night in jail.

That Thursday, hundreds of young people poured out of schoolhouse doors and windows. Finding schoolyard gates locked, they climbed over the fences. They made their way to the Sixteenth Street Baptist Church and then marched—back out of the church, down its broad steps, and into

above: A young demonstrator is hosed down as an armored vehicle races back and forth in an attempt to control the crowds.

opposite: On May 2, 1963, when children poured into Kelly Ingram Park, Bull and Birmingham's police department were ready for them with dogs and water hoses.

Kelly Ingram Park. All the while, Fred encouraged them and barked orders through a bullhorn from the top of the church steps.

Dr. King no longer had to worry about making up his mind. The children made his decision for him.

Bull was ready for the young marchers. He called out his police officers with their trained German shepherds. Other officers roared back and forth in a white armored car—a tank on wheels— and tried to corral the kids. The tank was Bull's latest weapon in fighting desegregation. From loudspeakers mounted atop the vehicle, the officers ordered kids to disperse. The children were pushed back from one area only to emerge from another, each time in greater numbers, as control of the park seesawed.

Wave after wave of children jammed into the elm-shaded square. Police with nightsticks began filling their paddy wagons with young protesters and hauling them to jail. By nightfall, more than

Police began filling their paddy wagons, and when those were filled to capacity, they brought in school buses to haul the young people away to jail or makeshift facilities at the fairgrounds.

one thousand children, some as young as seven, sat in Birmingham's jails. And Negroes who had been outraged at leaders for encouraging their children to march now turned their anger toward Bull Connor. In the days that followed, adults joined the demonstrations as the protests grew, and Dr. King, with Fred by his side, announced at a press conference, "The demonstrations will go on until some progress has been made."

By the end of the week, the police were forced to house arrested protesters in makeshift facilities at the fairgrounds. A local sheriff conceded that they'd run out of space.

Governor Wallace ordered the state highway patrol to Birmingham. After five weeks of racial strife in the city, he declared, "I am beginning to tire of agitators, integrationists, and others who seek to destroy law and order in Alabama."

Then on May 7, the protests seemed to get away from both Bull's police department and movement leaders as twenty-five hundred to three thousand

As the children's march wore on, the daily protests got away from the police and from the Project C leaders, but they prompted President John F. Kennedy to denounce segregation and to urge Congress to make the practice illegal.

demonstrators rampaged through the business district, taunting police and hurling stones. Bull deployed monitors—high-powered, tripod-mounted water cannons—each one fed by two 2½-inch hoses. He ordered the firemen to turn them on the protesters. And they did. The blasts of water sent demonstrators skittering head over heels across the sidewalks and over the grass with a force so powerful it took the bark off the trees. At one point, firemen lost control of a cannon. Its stream of water struck two police officers. One suffered fractured ribs; the other, a leg injury.

Firemen, on Bull's order, turn high-powered water cannons on the demonstrators. Later, a few fire fighters expressed remorse at following orders, but others seemed to enjoy it.

During the spring 1963 demonstrations, Eugene "Bull" Connor became the face of segregation, the face of everything that was evil in the South. But he'd played right into Fred's hands.

When firemen saw Fred at the top of the church steps, they turned the water on him, hurling him against the wall. He was carried away on a stretcher to an ambulance.

Hearing about the incident with Fred, Bull said he was sorry he'd missed it. "I wish they'd carried him away in a hearse." He must have been even more disappointed when Fred marched into the park later that day. This time he was leading another three hundred protesters, many of them children.

Since they began, the demonstrations were being captured by national-television crews and newspaper photographers. Fred's prophesy had come true: Bull had done something to further the cause of desegregation. His use of dogs and water cannons

As police tried to control the young demonstrators, white residents and their teenaged children watched from a distance.

had made him the symbol of Southern segregation and Klan hate. The white-owned afternoon newspaper appealed to President John F. Kennedy to negotiate a truce with the demonstration leaders.

The president's representatives tried to foster an agreement between the two sides. With Fred recuperating from injuries suffered by the blast of water, Dr. King agreed to call off the protests. When Fred learned about this, he was furious with the SCLC leader.

On May 8, 1963, Dr. King, with Fred and Abernathy at his side, announced that he was suspending demonstrations and that a settlement was near. Fred had not been consulted about the suspension of activities and was not in agreement. Even so, the demonstrations ended.

Always the actionist, Fred thought they should continue to apply pressure. But the marches ended, with Dr. King negotiating a scaled-back settlement that included a promise from white businessmen to desegregate lunch counters, drinking fountains, and bathrooms and to hire more black clerks in department stores. But the agreement lacked a timeline for implementation and relied mostly on the goodwill of the businessmen. Fred and many others were agitated that Dr. King had settled for less than immediate action and scrapped some of the movement's demands altogether. Even so, Fred read a prepared statement at a May 10 press conference—ironically, segregated—where he said

In fall 1963, as Birmingham prepared to integrate some of its schools, white students refused to attend classes and mounted their own protests. Here, students drive by West End High School dragging an effigy of a Negro at the side of their car.

Following the KKK bombing of the Sixteenth Street Baptist Church on September 15, 1963, Dr. King confers with Fred at a mass meeting of the ACMHR and Negro residents.

the Birmingham settlement offered to move all America a little closer to freedom and equality.

Project C was over.

On May 23, the Alabama Supreme Court ruled against Birmingham's commissioners. After almost eight weeks of confusion, the city finally had its new government, and Bull was out of a job. Mayor Boutwell and the city council removed the Colored Only signs over water fountains in June. In July, they voted to rescind the city's segregation laws.

As 1963 drew to a close, however, Birmingham and its people would see even darker days when the Klan detonated a Sunday morning bomb in September, under the steps of the Sixteenth Street Baptist Church, that claimed the lives of four innocent girls. It was the Klan's response to the desegregation of some of the city's schools. In the aftermath of the explosion, two more lives—young boys—would be cut short that day.

But the confrontations of spring 1963, the courage of Birmingham's young people to take to the streets and stand up to white oppression, and Fred's unyielding determination to achieve dignity through peaceful means all did their part to help push forward the sweeping equal rights legislation of 1964. Bull did his part, too, to further the cause of equality, just as Fred had predicted he would do. He and his entrenched attitudes about segregation were the perfect foils to Fred's quest for Negro justice.

In 1964, Bull ran for and was elected to two terms on the Public Service Commission (PSC), the statewide agency that regulated utilities. A stroke in 1966—the year Birmingham finally hired its first black police officer—left him confined to a wheelchair, but he decided to run for a third term on the PSC in 1972 and lost. On February 26, 1973, he suffered another stroke and, after lingering in the hospital for twelve days, died on March 10. Birmingham's unyielding voice of racism and segregation, the voice of Eugene "Bull" Connor, was stilled.

Fred returned to Cincinnati and Revelation Baptist Church, but he continued to keep his eyes on Birmingham and returned there often. In 1966, he organized a new church, Greater New Light Baptist in Cincinnati. As he had always done, he continued to let the Lord lead him in the fight for social and economic justice wherever it took him. His marching shoes always at the ready, he was the Reverend Fred L. Shuttlesworth—the man who spoke for Birmingham.

below left: **Bull Connor owed much of his political success to Fred Shuttlesworth, yet in the end his harsh attitudes proved to be his downfall.**

below right: **In 1961, CBS reporter Howard K. Smith filmed a special piece called "Who Speaks for Birmingham?" It was Reverend Fred L. Shuttlesworth who spoke for Birmingham, whether in that city or in Cincinnati.**

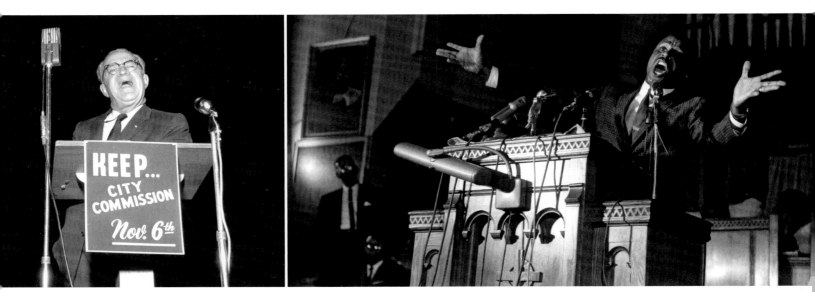

I **first** encountered Reverend Fred L. Shuttlesworth's name while researching an earlier book, *Birmingham Sunday*. In reading about the events leading up to that tragic day in September when the Ku Klux Klan detonated a dynamite bomb outside the Sixteenth Street Baptist Church, I came to realize that the Birmingham campaign for dignity and equality was spearheaded by one man, a gutsy preacher from Bethel Baptist Church.

Without Fred Shuttlesworth, the Birmingham campaign and the role Reverend Dr. Martin Luther King, Jr., played in it may have taken a vastly different shape. It was Fred who urged a reluctant Dr. King to shine the light of the Southern Christian Leadership Conference on the city. It was Fred who planned strategy and provided soldiers from the Alabama Christian Movement for Human Rights for local demonstrations, even as Dr. King was the national voice of the civil rights movement. Fred's actions in the 1950s and 1960s helped pave the way to the landmark Civil Rights Act of 1964 and Voting Rights Act of 1965. I wanted to know more

about this charismatic leader whose faith led him to stand up to white supremacists and look death in the face without so much as flinching.

Fred was a fighter who believed that the best defense was to "harass the harassers" through nonviolent direct action. But his years of social activism were not without controversy and cost. His frequent absences from the pulpit left some of his parishioners feeling neglected and angry—as if they weren't getting their Sunday offering's worth. His dictatorial leadership of the ACMHR led even some of his closest allies to challenge his authority. When they voiced their unhappiness, he confronted it the same way he took on segregation—by direct action. He'd call for a vote of support, vowing to step down if it wasn't forthcoming. This tactic silenced the grumblers and left him free to go about the business of defeating Jim Crow segregation.

His social activism also took a toll on Ruby (b. 1922). The couple's twenty-nine-year marriage was often a stormy one with disagreements erupting over their fishbowl existence, the constant threat of Klan violence, and their perpetual lack of money. The couple divorced in

1970. On February 1, 1971, Ruby died of heart failure after years of poor health. Their children all became teachers.

In the 1980s, Fred founded the Shuttlesworth Housing Foundation to assist low-income Cincinnatians in purchasing their first homes. In January 2001, President Bill Clinton honored him with the Presidential Citizens Medal, the second-highest honor given to a private citizen. He retired from the ministry just shy of his eighty-fourth birthday in 2006 and married Sephira Bailey later the same year. She had helped nurse him back to health following removal of a benign brain tumor in 2005. After his retirement, he traveled the country lecturing about civil- and human-rights

President Bill Clinton on the day he awarded the Presidential Citizens Medal to Fred in 2001.

issues until September 2007, when he suffered a stroke. Awarded a dozen honorary degrees from colleges and universities in recognition of his lifelong commitment to racial justice and equality, Fred returned to Birmingham in 2008. The city where so many once scorned him extended its welcome home by renaming the airport Birmingham-Shuttlesworth International Airport.

Eugene "Bull" Connor was an enigma to me. He professed no interest in politics. Yet, except for a brief period in the 1950s after a grand jury investigation recommended his impeachment following accusations of improper behavior with his secretary, he continually sought one political office or another from 1934 until shortly before his death in 1973. While most of his campaigns were victorious, he also knew defeat. He ran losing races for governor in 1950 and 1962. He ran for and lost his bid to become sheriff of Jefferson County (Birmingham) in 1954. In 1963, he failed to win a recommendation for appointment to the State Pardon-Parole Board.

Throughout his political career, Bull courted controversy. He walked out of the 1948 Democratic National Convention

as he and other Alabama delegates had pledged to do if a pro-civil-rights candidate was selected. Harry Truman was chosen to be the Democratic candidate. Truman urged a strong civil rights platform because it appalled him that African American soldiers, who had fought for and defended the United States in World War II, were arriving home by bus in the South only to be beaten by Klansmen. Also in 1948, Bull arrested Senator Glen H. Taylor of Idaho when he came to Birmingham to address the Southern Negro Youth Congress and entered the meeting through the door marked Colored. As the years progressed, Bull's attitudes about segregation only intensified, and he is oft quoted as insisting that "[w]hite and Negro are not to segregate together." (Some historians and archivists doubt the authenticity of this contradictory quotation.) By 1963 he had become, through his actions, the caricature of a Southern redneck and, by the time of his death, a man out of step with the mainstream of American society.

For all their differences, Bull and Fred shared things in common. Both men came from humble backgrounds. Each

Bull Connor addresses a 1948 meeting of the States Rights delegates in Birmingham. Earlier he led half the Alabama contingent out of the Democratic National Convention over the party's stand on civil rights.

wanted to leave behind his vision of an improved Birmingham for the next generation. For Bull, this meant preserving the Southern way of life and all that entailed, while for Fred it embodied racial justice and equality of opportunity. Perhaps their biggest similarity was each man's doggedness. And it was this trait that proved to be Bull's political undoing and his downfall. For Fred, his determined persistence, coupled with an abiding faith that he was following God's plan, worked with his goal to make Birmingham's powerful elite reconsider the cost of segregation.

Theophilus Eugene "Bull" Connor, with his wife and daughter, was a colorful Southern politician without whom Fred's struggle to bring equality to Birmingham's Negroes might have gone on even longer than it did. Bull never softened his stance about segregation.

Throughout the main text of this book, and with the greatest respect, I referred to African Americans as black, Negro, and colored. These were the terms in common use at the time, and the terms that Fred himself used.

A mountain of sources was used for reference. I am indebted to all those who told Fred's and Bull's stories in books published before this one. I am most grateful to Fred himself for being the courageous, confrontational, hardheaded leader he was. It was my great honor to meet and spend some time with him in the spring of 2010. Although he was in frail health, the fire of a life well lived shone brightly in his eyes. His reminiscences with Dr. Horace Huntley for the Birmingham Civil Rights Institute's *Oral History Project* and with Dr. Andrew M. Manis for his *Oral History Interviews*, part of the Birmingham Public Library's Department of Archives and Manuscripts, were immensely helpful for drawing quotations and gaining insight. For scope and sequence, three titles were indispensable: *A Fire You Can't Put Out: The Civil Rights Life of Birmingham's Reverend Fred Shuttlesworth* by Andrew M. Manis; *Fred Shuttlesworth: Civil Rights Actionist* by William A. Nunnelley; and *Bull Connor* by William A. Nunnelley. Also helpful were *Birmingham Revolutionaries: The Reverend Fred Shuttlesworth and the Alabama Christian Movement for Human Rights*, edited by Marjorie L. White and Andrew M. Manis; and *A Walk to Freedom: The Reverend Fred Shuttlesworth and the Alabama Christian Movement for Human Rights, 1956–1964*, compiled by Marjorie L. White. I believe I have an obligation to acknowledge Bull Connor, not out of respect for his thoughts or deeds, which were immoral and criminal, but because he was the perfect foe for Fred and his allies. Without this staunch racist and his harsh response to the African American cry for justice, civil rights progress might have taken an even longer time in coming.

Reverend Fred L. Shuttlesworth never once thought about giving up the fight for human and civil rights. He was, after all, following the path God intended for him, and he'd answered that calling early in his life.

For Further Information

Bausum, Ann. *Freedom Riders: John Lewis and Jim Zwerg on the Front Lines of the Civil Rights Movement*. Washington, DC: National Geographic Children's Books, 2006.

Brimner, Larry Dane. *Birmingham Sunday*. Honesdale, PA: Calkins Creek, 2010.

Brimner, Larry Dane. *We Are One: The Story of Bayard Rustin*. Honesdale, PA: Calkins Creek, 2007.

Freedman, Russell. *Freedom Walkers: The Story of the Montgomery Bus Boycott*. New York: Holiday House, 2006.

Hampton, Henry. *Eyes on the Prize: America's Civil Rights Movement*. Boston: Blackside, Inc. PBS Video, 2006. DVD.

Hoose, Phillip. *Claudette Colvin: Twice Toward Justice*. New York: Melanie Kroupa/Farrar, Straus Giroux, 2009.

Mayer, Robert H. *When the Children Marched: The Birmingham Civil Rights Movement*. Berkeley Heights, NJ: Enslow, 2008.

Miller, Calvin Craig. *No Easy Answers: Bayard Rustin and the Civil Rights Movement*. Greensboro, NC: Morgan Reynolds, 2005.

Partridge, Elizabeth. *Marching for Freedom: Walk Together, Children, and Don't You Grow Weary*. New York: Viking, 2009.

Pinkney, Andrea Davis. *Sit-In: How Four Friends Stood Up by Sitting Down*. Illustrated by Brian Pinkney. New York: Little, Brown, 2010.

Waxman, Laura Hamilton. *Coretta Scott King*. Minneapolis: Lerner Publications, 2008.

Weatherford, Carole Boston. *Birmingham, 1963*. Honesdale, PA: Wordsong, 2007.

Acknowledgments

Although the act of writing is usually solitary, the process of uncovering information so that writing may be pursued often requires an ensemble cast. I am indebted to many people for their assistance, encouragement, support, suggestions, and patience. Chief among them are Laura Anderson, archivist at the Birmingham Civil Rights Institute; James L. Baggett, archivist, Birmingham Public Library, Department of Archives and Manuscripts; Linda McFarland, librarian, Birmingham Public Library, Microfilm Department; everyone in the Birmingham Public Library's Southern History and Government Documents departments; Dr. Horace Huntley, former professor of history, University of Alabama at Birmingham, for fact-checking my manuscript; J. Edmund Odum, Jr., attorney, for clippings about his father's prosecution of Bull following Bull's arrest for alleged improper conduct with his secretary; Voncille Williams, *The Birmingham News*, Photo Department; Bessemer Hall of History Museum, for resolving image questions; Anniston Public Library, for responding to e-mail and quickly tracking down information; Betty Shuttlesworth Williams, for her hospitality and assistance with family photos; Joan and Neal Broerman, for friendship, encouragement, and introductions; Kent L. Brown Jr., founder, Boyds Mills Press, for his support; Carolyn P. Yoder, editor, for her faith and patience; Joan Hyman, Robbin Gourley, and Bill Anton | Service Station, part of the Calkins Creek editorial and design team; and finally Reverend Fred L. and Sephira Bailey Shuttlesworth, for opening their hearts and sharing their time and thoughts with me so that Fred's story could be told.

page 7
"I have a feeling ...": Reverend Fred L. Shuttlesworth, interview by Horace B. Huntley, Ph.D., December 10, 1996, *Oral History Project*, transcript (Tape 1), Birmingham Civil Rights Institute, p. 23.

page 9
"like Moses ...": Fred Shuttlesworth, interview by Andrew M. Manis, *Andrew M. Manis Oral History Interviews*, transcript (File #1437.2.1), Department of Archives and Manuscripts, Birmingham Public Library, p. 10.

page 12
"[c]orn, 'tatoes, ...": Fred Shuttlesworth, *Oral History Project*, (Tape 1), p. 9.

"My mother never ...": Ibid., p. 3.

"about the ...": Ibid., p. 4.

page 13
"She didn't have ...": Ibid., p. 5.

page 14
"budget was ...": Ibid., p. 15.

page 17
"[Y]ou don't know ...": Ibid., December 10, 1996, transcript (Tape 2), p. 14.

page 18
"[I]t is people ...": Fred Shuttlesworth, *Andrew M. Manis Oral History Interviews*, transcript (File #1437.2.2), p. 15.

"[M]aybe your little ...": Fred Shuttlesworth, December 10, 1996, *Oral History Project*, transcript (Tape 3), p. 3.

page 19
"[I]t was almost ...": Ibid., p. 1.

"was the biggest ...": Ibid.

"We thought that ...": Ibid.

page 20
"a desire to push ...": Fred Shuttlesworth, *Andrew M. Manis Oral History Interviews*, (File #1437.2.2), pp. 19–20.

page 22
"[t]hat religion ought ...": Ibid., (File #1437.2.4), pp. 21–22.

page 24
"Negro policemen ...": Ibid., (File #1437.2.2), p. 20.

"We nicknamed ...": Ibid., (File #1437.2.1), p. 1.

"officials could ...": Ibid.

page 25
"[W]ell, somebody ...": Fred Shuttlesworth, *Oral History Project*, (Tape 3), p. 8.

"must do ...": Fred Shuttlesworth, *Andrew M. Manis Oral History Interviews*, transcript (File #1437.2.4), p. 19.

"'I'm ... willing ...'": Fred Shuttlesworth, *Oral History Project*, (Tape 3), p. 8.

"that God ...": Ibid.

"[He] told me ...": Ibid., pp. 10, 11.

page 26
"outlaw the will ...": Ibid., p. 10.

"to challenge ...": Ibid., p. 12.

"[S]omehow ... , Nelson Smith ...": Ibid., p. 16.

"I said to Nelson ...": Ibid.

page 27
"rise": Ibid.

"Whoom!": Ibid., p. 17.

page 28
"'Reverend, I guess ...'": Ibid., p. 18.

"[W]hen the blast ...": Fred Shuttlesworth, *Andrew M. Manis Oral History Interviews*, (File #1437.2.2), p. 25.

"'Reverend, I'm so sorry ...'": Fred Shuttlesworth, *Oral History Project*, (Tape 3), p. 18.

"Officer, you are ...": Ibid.

page 29
"We [are going to] do ...": Ibid., p. 20.

"[The] Klan made ...": Ibid., p. 21.

page 33
"sole motive ...": Deputy Tom Ellison, "Man Mutilated to Prove Klan Worth, Claim," *Birmingham News*, September 9, 1957.

page 35
"The men attacked ...": Nathaniel Lee, "Negro Beaten at Phillips High," *Birmingham News*, September 9, 1957.

"'[A]w, you ...'": Fred Shuttlesworth, *Oral History Project*, (Tape 3), p. 26.

page 36
"I think they ...": Ibid.

"'Reverend, I'm so ...'": Ibid., pp. 27–28.

"Well, doctor, the ...": Ibid., p. 28.

"[N]o more problems ...": Ibid.

page 37
"[N]either official ...": Fred Shuttlesworth, "Negro Beaten at Phillips High," *Birmingham News*, September 9, 1957.

"I'm not mad ...": Fred Shuttlesworth, December 11, 1996, *Oral History Project*, transcript (Tape 4), p. 6.

page 38
"[W]e don't need ...": Eugene "Bull" Connor, "'Agitators' Face Jail, Connor Says," *Birmingham News*, October 28, 1958.

page 41
"the law ...": unnamed source, "Fear and Hatred Grip Birmingham," by Harrison E. Salisbury, *New York Times*, April 12, 1960.

Websites active at time of publication

"We will take …": Mayor James W. Morgan, "Connor Asks Negro Pastor to Take Lie Test in Bombing," *Birmingham News*, June 3, 1958.

"I don't think …": Fred Shuttlesworth, Ibid.

"I am going …": Bull Connor, Ibid.

page 43
"I got a whole lot …": Bull Connor, "'Just a Good Old Country Boy'— Bull," *Birmingham News*, October 18, 1931.

"I went crazy …": Ibid.

"[M]y wife and I …": Ibid.

page 48
"death's jaws": Fred Shuttlesworth, *Oral History Project*, (Tape 4), p. 1.

"God wouldn't …": Ibid.

"couldn't be …": Ibid., p. 7.

page 49
"I accept …": Fred Shuttlesworth, "Shuttlesworth Returns Challenge of Connor," by George Cook, *Birmingham Post-Herald*, June 4, 1958.

page 50
"I waited …": Bull Connor, "Negroes Routed by Police at Birmingham," by Claude Sitton, *New York Times*, May 8, 1963.

page 51
"Mr. Conn[o]r, …": Fred Shuttlesworth, December 10, 1996, *Oral History Project*, transcript (Tape 5), p. 6.

page 56
"It is disturbing …": Bull Connor, "No Time for Racial Agitation, Says Connor," *Birmingham Post-Herald*, July 23, 1958.

"I don't believe …": Ibid.

"scouring the town …": Ibid.

"raising money …": Ibid.

"[t]he 'pressure, …'": Fred Shuttlesworth, Ibid.

page 57
"I personally do …": Ibid.

"not led to the bombing …": Ibid.

"Negro stenographers, …": Ibid.

page 58
"Never set …": Fred Shuttlesworth, *Andrew M. Manis Oral History Interviews*, (File #1437.2.2), p. 30.

page 59
"this is …": Fred Shuttlesworth, *Oral History Project*, (Tape 4), p. 13.

"solemnly promised …": Fred Shuttlesworth, *Andrew M. Manis Oral History Interviews*, (File #1437.2.2), p. 31.

"They sat …": Ibid.

page 61
"Damn the law …": Bull Connor, *The New York Times Company v. Eugene Connor*, transcript, U.S. Court of Appeals Fifth Circuit, August 4, 1996 (paragraph 33, 43), bulk.resource.org/courts.gov/c/F2/365/365.F2d.567.22362_1.html (accessed June 15, 2010).

page 75
"'I got …'": Fred Shuttlesworth, *Oral History Project*, (Tape 5), p. 0.

"doctor,": Ibid.

"[N]o, there …": Fred Shuttlesworth, *Oral History Project*, (Tape 5), p. 4.

"I have decided …": Ibid.

"[N]ow you are …": Ibid.

page 76
"[S]egregation today …": George C. Wallace, "The 1963 Inaugural Address of Governor George C. Wallace," January 14, 1963, transcript, Alabama Department of Archives and History, archives. state.al.us/govs_list/inaugural speech.html, p. 5 (accessed July 10, 2010).

page 87
"unwise and …": "The Following Is the Public Statement Directed to Martin Luther King, Jr., by Eight Alabama Clergymen," April 12, 1963, Priests for Life, priestsforlife.org/articles/kingltroriginal.htm (accessed June 25, 2010).

page 93
"The demonstrations …": Martin Luther King, Jr., "Rioting Negroes Routed by Police at Birmingham," by Claude Sitton, *New York Times*, May 8, 1963.

page 94
"I am beginning …": George C. Wallace, Ibid.

page 96
"I wish …": Bull Connor, Ibid.

page 102
"harass the harassers": Fred Shuttlesworth, *Andrew M. Manis Oral History Interviews*, (File #1437.2.2), p. 30.

page 103
"[w]hite and Negro …": Bull Connor, "Fear and Hatred Grip Birmingham," by Harrison E. Salisbury, *New York Times*, April 12, 1960.

page 111
"[o]ne of the great …": John F. Kennedy, "Notes on Situation in Birmingham, Alabama, 05/12/1963," from Collection JFK-POF: Papers of John F. Kennedy: President's Office Files, 01/20/1961–11/22/1963, John F. Kennedy Library, Boston, Massachusetts, U.S. National Archives and Records Administration (ARC Identifier 193803), archives.gov (accessed February 21, 2011).

Index

Page numbers in **boldface** refer to photographs and/or captions.

A

Aaron, Edward Judge, 33–34, 37
Abernathy, Ralph, 75, **86**, 86–87, **97**
ACMHR-SCLC spring demonstrations, 76–88
Alabama Christian Movement for Human Rights (ACMHR), **endsheet facing title page**, **2–3**, 28–30, **29**, 34–35, **36**, **37**, 46–49, 58, 60, 68, 70–71, 75–76, 79, 82, 84, **100**, 102; Communist ties, 55–57; founding of, 26, **26**; newsletter, 64
Alabama State College for Negroes, 16, 61
Anniston, Alabama, 65–66, 67, 71

B

Belafonte, Harry, 60, 61
Bethel Baptist Church, 17–19, 20–21, 22, **27**, 32, 49, 54, 55, 76, 102
Bevel, James, 88, 89, **89**, 90
Birmingham Manifesto, 79
Boutwell, Albert, 77, 79, 83, 100
Bradley, Wade, 21
Brown v. Board of Education decision. See *Oliver L. Brown et al. versus the Board of Education of Topeka (Kansas)*

C

Cedar Grove Academy, 15
Children's march, **90**, 90–100, **91**, **92**, **93**, **94**, **95**
Christmas night bombing, 1956, 9–11, **27**, 27–28, **28**, 30, 41–42, 48–49, 53
Clinton, Bill, 102, **102**
Communism, 56, 57, 74
Congress of Racial Equality (CORE), 63, **66**
Connor, Beara (Levens), 43, **44**, 45, **104**
Connor, Dora Jean, **44**, 45, **104**

Connor, Hugh King, 42
Connor, Molly, 42
Connor, Theophilus Eugene "Bull," **2–3**, 35, **38–39**, 38–49, **40**, **43**, **44**, **45**, **46**, **47**, 50, 53–56, 57, 58–62, 65–67, 69–74, 76–77, **77**, 79, **80**, 82–84, **85**, 87–88, 91, **91**, 93, 95–96, **96**, 100–101, **101**, 103, **103**, 104, **104**, 105
Corinthian Baptist Church, 15

D

Daniel Payne College, 59
Declaration of Constitutional Principles, 25
Democratic National Convention, 1948, 103, **103**
Dukes, Frank, 72

E

Ellison, Tom, 33

F

Fellowship of Reconciliation (FOR), 63
First Baptist Church (Selma), 16
Foley, Albert, 83
Freedom Rides, 63–68, 70

G

Gandhi, Mohandas K., 61, 63
Gaston, A. G., 74–75, **75**
George, Walter F., 25
Great Depression, 12
Greater New Light Baptist Church, 101
Greene, Vetter, 11
Grooms, Harlan H., 58, 67, 70, 71

H

Hall, Will, 54
Hendricks, Lola, 79
Hill, Ambus, 79
Hoover, J. Edgar, 66
Horne, Lena, 61

J

James, Earl D., 60
Jim Crow laws, 20, **20**, 22, 25, 26, **28**, 47, 48, 58, 60, 62, **62**, 71, 76, **80**, 82, 102
Johnson, Stone, 54

Jones, Walter B., 24
Journey of Reconciliation, 63

K

Kennedy, John F., **94**, 97, **110–111**, **112**
Kennedy, Robert F., 67
King, Alfred D., 85
King, Martin Luther, Jr., 32, 59, 61, 74–76, 79, 83, 85, **86**, 86–88, 91, 93, 97, **97**, **100**, 102, **112**
Ku Klux Klan (KKK), **8**, 9, 22, 23, 27–29, **28**, 33–34, 36–37, 42, 46, 49, **52**, 53–54, 63, 65–66, **66**, 68, 70, 74, 83, 90, 97, 100, **100**, 102, 103, **112**

L

Lee, Nathaniel, 35
"Letter from Birmingham Jail," 88
Lie detector challenge, 41–42, 49, 53, 55
Lindbergh, Robert E., 21, 47
Lucy, Autherine, 22–24, **23**

M

Marshall, Thurgood, 22, **23**
McCarthy, Joseph R., 57
Miles College, 59, 72
Montgomery bus boycott, 22, 24, 26–27, 32, 61
Moore, Jamie, 65, 84, **84**
Morgan, James W., 21, **40**, 41
Morris, William Hugh, 53, 55
Motley, D. L., Sr., 17
Myers, Pollie Anne, 22–23

N

National Association for the Advancement of Colored People (NAACP), 18, 22–26, **23**, **26**, 56, 57
New Pilgrim Baptist Church, 26
New York Times, 60–61

O

Oliver L. Brown et al. versus the Board of Education of Topeka (Kansas), 19, 20, 22–23, 25, 30, 32

P

Palm Sunday march, 85–86, **86**
Parker, Ralph E., 30, 31

Parks, Rosa, 22
Patterson, John, 24, **40**, 61, 67
Peck, James, 63, 65–66, **66**
Phifer, J. S., 35–36
Phillips High School, 33–35, **35**, **36**, 37, 48
Porter, John T., 85
Presidential Citizens Medal, 102, **102**
Project "C," **79**, 79–100, **89**, **94**

R

Revelation Missionary Baptist Church, 68–69, 101
Robey, Lucinda B., 25, **26**
Robinson, Charlie, 10, **27**, 27–28
Robinson, March, 11
Robinson, Martha, 11
Russell, Richard, 25
Rustin, Bayard, 60, 61

S

Salisbury, Harrison E., 61
Sardis Missionary Baptist Church, 25
Selective-buying campaign, 72–73, 85
Selma University, 15, 23
Shores, Arthur, 22–23, 25, 30
Shuttlesworth, Alberta (Robinson), **11**, 11–13, **12**
Shuttlesworth, Carolyn, 10, **10**, 16
Shuttlesworth, Cleola (Robinson), 11
Shuttlesworth, Eugene, 12
Shuttlesworth, Fred, Jr., 10, **10**, 15
Shuttlesworth, Fred L., **6–7**, 9–23, **10**, **17**, 24, 25, 41–42, 53–55, 70–72, 74–76, **100**, 100–104, **101**, **102**, **104**; Alabama Christian Movement for Human Rights, role in, 26, **26**, 29–30, 46–47, 48–49, 55–59, 71; Christmas-night bombing, 9–11, 27–28, **28**, **29**, 41–42, 53; Cincinnati, move to, 69–70; Freedom Rides, 63–68, **64**, **66**, 67, **68**; Greensboro sit-ins, 59–60; lawsuits against, 60–61; Phillips

High incident, 32–37, **35**, **37**, 48; Project C, 79, 82–100, **84**, **86**, **97**; Revelation Missionary Baptist Church, 68, 69–70; Terminal Station integration, 31–32, **32**
Shuttlesworth, Patricia Ann, 9–10, **10**, 14, 15, 33, **35**, **36**, **37**
Shuttlesworth, Ruby Fredericka "Ricky," 10, **10**, 15, 33, 35, **35**
Shuttlesworth, Ruby Keeler, 10, **13**, 13–14, 31, 32, **32**, 35, 36, 48, 69, 102; Terminal Station integration, 31–32, **32**
Shuttlesworth Housing Foundation, 102
Sit-in movement, 59–60, 82, 84, **84**
Sixteenth Street Baptist Church, 84, 86, 89, 90, 100, **100**, 102
Smith, Howard K., 68, **101**
Smith, Nelson H., Jr., 26, 85
Smyer, Sidney, 74–75
Southern Christian Leadership Conference (SCLC), 32, 59–60, 74–76, 79, 84, 88, 97
Southern Manifesto, 25
Stoner, Jesse Benjamin "J.B.," Jr., **52**, 53–55
Sullivan, L. B., 60–61

T

Taylor, Glen H., 103
Terminal Station, 31–32, **32**
Thurmond, Strom, 25
Till, Emmett Louis, 21, **21**

U

Union of Soviet Socialist Republics (USSR), 56–57
University of Alabama, Tuscaloosa, 22–24

W

Walker, Wyatt Tee, 79, 84, 88
Wallace, George C., 73, **73**, 76, **77**, 94
Washington, Booker T., 14
Weaver, Lamar, 31
Wilson, Walter, 35
World War II, 14, 56, 57, 103

Picture Credits

One of the great moral
issues of our time is the
achievement of equal
opportunity for all citizens
Too long have Negroes
been denied ~~their~~ fair ~~and~~
~~equal~~ treatment and equal
opportunity in all parts of
our land. It is
increasingly clear that this
injustice will no longer be
tolerated by them as it should not
be tolerated by any American.

These are not problems of Birmingham, the South or Negroes. They are problems which must concern all of us and which all of us have a moral obligation to put right.

Last week the citizens of Birmingham faced up to that obligation. All of us should be grateful to them for doing so.

In the end, Fred was right about Birmingham and about Bull Connor. By persistently challenging this Southern city's second-class treatment of blacks, and standing up to Bull's intolerance, Fred began to see a change in attitudes about civil rights in that city and across the nation. Following the events of spring 1963, President John F. Kennedy urged Congress to pass legislation that would guarantee equality for all of America's citizens, calling it "[o]ne of the great moral issues of our time . . ." in handwritten notes he made in preparation for a public statement about the situation in Birmingham.

Fred's stand against Bull Connor and the Klan in Birmingham helped bring about national change when President Lyndon B. Johnson signed the 1964 Civil Rights Act, first introduced by President John F. Kennedy. Reverend Dr. Martin Luther King, Jr., and other dignitaries look on.